GLOBE FEARON

LITERATURE

COMPREHENSION AND VOCABULARY WORKBOOK

▪ *Purple Level* ▪

GLOBE FEARON
Pearson Learning Group

Supervising Editors: Karen McCollum and Rosely Himmelstein
Editor: Ayanna Taylor
Editorial Developer: Pearson Education Development Group
Production Editor: Travis Bailey
Designer: Angel Weyant
Manufacturing Supervisor: Mark Cirillo

Acknowledgments: (p.4) "Love" from 3000 Years of Black Poetry. Translated by Raoul Abdul from the Raoul Abdul Collection used by permission of the Buxton National Historic Site & Museum. (p.16) "Here—Hold My Hand" from I am a Black Woman, published by Wm. Morrow & Co., 1970, used by permission of the author. (p.16) "Greyday" from Oh Pray My Wings Are Gonna Fit Me Well by Maya Angelou. Copyright © 1975 by Maya Angelou. Reprinted by permission of Random House. (p.18)"Housecleaning" from The Selected Poems of Nikki Giovanni by Nikki Giovanni compilation copyright © 1996 by Nikki Giovanni. Reprinted by permission of HarperCollins Publishers, Inc. William Morrow. (p. 22) "Troubled Island" by Langston Hughes and William Grant Still. Copyright © 1976 by Southern Music Publishing Co., Inc. International Copyright Secured. Used by permission. (p.34)"hist, whist." Copyright 1923, 1951, © 1991 by the Trustees for the E. E. Cummings Trust. Copyright © 1976 by George James Firmage, from Complete Poems: 1904-1962 by E. E. Cummings, edited by George J. Firmage. Used by permission of Liveright Publishing Corporation. (p. 38)"The Listeners" from The Collected Poems of Walter de la Mare by Walter de la Mare. The Literary Trustees of Walter de la Mare, and the Society of Authors as their representatives. (p.56)"Displays of Skill: The Bat" (retitled "The Bat") from Nature and Love Poems, copyright © 1969 by Ruth Hershberger, published by Eakins Press. (p.78)"Dreams" from Collected Poems by Langston Hughes. Copyright © 1994 by the Estate of Langston Hughes. Reprinted by permission of Alfred A. Knopf, a Division of Random House Inc. (p.78)"Sympathy" from Black Writers of America by Paul Dunbar. Prentice Hall Inc. (p.90)"Song of Failure" from Literature of the American Indians by Juanita Platero & Siyowin Miller. Published by Glencoe Press. (p.90)"War Song" from Literature of the American Indians by Juanita Platero & Siyowin Miller. Published by Glencoe Press. (p.90)"Warrior Song II" from Literature of the American Indians by Juanita Platero & Siyowin Miller. Published by Glencoe Press. (p.104)"Some People" reprinted with the permission of Simon & Schuster Books for Young Readers, an imprint of Simon & Schuster Children's Publishing Division from Poems by Rachel Field (Macmillan, NY, 1957). (p.108)"Whale Hunting" by Sally Nashookpuk from Here I Am! by Virginia Olsen Baron. Copyright © 1969 by Virginia Olsen Baron. Used by permission of Dutton Children's Books, a division of Penguin Putnam Inc. (p.108) "Luther Leavitt" by Alfred Brower from Here I Am! by Virginia Olsen Baron. Copyright © 1969 by Virginia Olsen Baron. Used by permission of Dutton Children's Books, a division of Penguin Putnam Inc.

ISBN 0-130-23550-4
Printed in the United States of America
4 5 6 7 8 9 10 07 06 05 04 03

Globe Fearon
Pearson Learning Group

1-800-321-3106
www.pearsonlearning.com

CONTENTS

UNIT 1 LOOKING AT LOVE

UNIT 2 THE UNKNOWN

**may have been titled "The Loch Ness Monster" in previous printings*

UNIT 3 SUSPENSE

UNIT 4 DISCOVERIES

UNIT 5 HEROES

UNIT 6 GENERATIONS

Name ______________________ Date ______________

THE LOCKET/THE KISS

Word List

ardently	**Confederate**	**consolations**	**guile**
insolent	**musket**	**perturbed**	**relent**
resignation	**sanctified**	**semblance**	**stammered**
suffused			

I. Write a word from the Word List to match each definition.

1. with great enthusiasm ______________
2. greatly disturbed ______________
3. a supporter of the South, during the Civil War ______________
4. spread through ______________
5. the use of cunning; slyness ______________
6. rude or insulting ______________
7. to become more compassionate ______________
8. unintentionally repeated the same sound ______________
9. outward appearance ______________
10. set apart as holy ______________

II. Complete each of the following sentences with a word from the Word List.

1. The neighbors offered their ______________ to the family of the accident victim.
2. The girl accepted her illness with quiet ______________.
3. The frightened soldier dropped his ______________ as he ran away, leaving him defenseless.
4. Melissa ______________ believed that her friend was the best athlete on the team.
5. When it seemed that their team might lose the championship, the fans became ______________.

Name ______________________________ *Date* ______________

The Locket/The Kiss

Draw Conclusions

Writers often reveal a character's emotions through the character's actions. For example, read this excerpt from "The Locket":

> . . . she folded the letter and put it back in the desk. Already she gave herself a modest little air like her Aunt Tavie. She walked with a slow glide, unconsciously imitating Mademoiselle Tavie, whom some youthful sorrow had robbed of earthly joys while leaving her with the illusions of youth.

You can make the logical conclusion that Octavie has accepted her loss and has gone into mourning. Her saving the letter and giving herself "a modest little air like her Aunt Tavie" support that conclusion. However, it is illogical to conclude that she is angry about her loss, since there are no details to support that idea.

Use this excerpt from "The Kiss" to determine if the conclusions below are logical or illogical. Support your choices with details from the excerpt.

> During one of the pauses between their talk of the last tea and the next party, the door opened. A young man whom Brantain knew quite well entered. The girl turned her face toward him. A stride or two brought him to her side, and he bent over her chair. Before she could suspect what he would do, for she did not realize that he had not seen her visitor, he pressed a warm kiss upon her lips.
>
> Brantain slowly arose. The girl arose, too, but quickly. The newcomer stood between them, a little amusement and some challenge struggling with the confusion in his face.

1. The young man and the girl know each other quite well.

____

____

2. The young man wants to destroy the developing relationship between the girl and Brantain.

____

____

Name ______________________________ *Date* ______________

LOVE

Word List

love	**shaped**	**gizzard**
lizard	**tickle**	**fall**

I. Write a word from the Word List that matches each definition.

1. type of reptile ____________
2. touch that makes someone laugh ____________
3. to drop down freely ____________
4. humorous word for stomach ____________
5. formed or outlined ____________
6. intense affection ____________

II. Decide whether the italicized word in each sentence is a noun (N) or a verb (V) and write the appropriate letter.

____ 1. I have a *tickle* in my throat.

____ 2. Ron says that horseback riding is his greatest *love.*

____ 3. I'm afraid that I will *fall* off my skis before I reach the bottom of the hill.

____ 4. Tina took a bad *fall* down the stairs.

____ 5. I *love* my boyfriend Jake; maybe some day we will get married.

III. Write two words that rhyme with each word listed below.

1. love ____________ ____________
2. fall ____________ ____________
3. shaped ____________ ____________
4. lizard ____________ ____________
5. tickle ____________ ____________

Name ______________________ *Date* ______________

LOVE

Understand Idioms

An idiom is an expression that has a meaning different from the dictionary meanings of its words. For example, read this excerpt from "Love."

> But the great fall is
> When you fall in love.

The last line contains an idiom—"fall in love." If you looked up the meaning of each word in this idiom, the meaning would be "to drop physically into affection." But this idiom, or expression, means "to become in love" with someone.

Underline the idiom in each of these poems. Write the meaning of each idiom on the lines below.

1. Spring is in the air.
You can feel it everywhere.

____

____

2. Say it isn't true.
Yesterday we jumped for joy because of our love
Today we cry these tears for the same reason.

____

____

3. I finally decided to say it out loud.
To you, out loud
"I love you." It was easy to say.
And then you say
To me, out loud.
"Let's call it quits."
Was it as easy?

____

____

Name ______________________ Date ____________

First Person Demonstrative

Word List

posy	gristle	gripe
heave	crawl	poison ivy
long	tease	wrench

I. Write the word from the Word List that best matches each definition.

1. tough, elastic white animal tissue ____________
2. move on hands and knees ____________
3. back-comb hair so it stands up ____________
4. to cause sharp pain in the bowels ____________
5. itchy weed ____________
6. a flower or bouquet ____________
7. throw ____________
8. pull ____________

II. Complete each sentence with a word from the Word List.

1. I ____________ to hold your hand.
2. She gave a ____________ to each bridesmaid to carry.
3. This meat is hard to chew because it has a lot of ____________ in it.
4. If you reach too far with a tennis racket, you can ____________ your shoulder.
5. Only the smallest boy was able to ____________ through the window.
6. You'll itch all week if you touch that ____________!
7. Anne decided she wouldn't ____________ her hair again.
8. The athlete had to ____________ the shot-put as far as he could.

Name ______________________________ Date ______________

First Person Demonstrative

Understand Figurative Language

Figures of speech are used in all types of literature. One of the common figures of speech is hyperbole, or exaggeration. When a writer wants to stress a particular idea, exaggeration is often a creative way to do so.

For each sentence below, write the words that make up the hyperbole.

1. The highway continued in a never-ending line.

____

2. Her beauty is eternal; it will never fade.

____

3. The eagle climbed so high it was close to the sun.

____

4. The athlete's heart beat as loudly as a drum.

____

5. She had the biggest eyes.

____

6. There was no better friend in the entire world.

____

7. The elephant's trunk squirted water like a fire hydrant.

____

8. He is as strong as an ox.

____

9. I'd rather gather a posy of poison ivy than ask if you love me.

____

10. The boy was so hungry he could eat a horse.

____

Name ______________________________ Date ______________

WHAT IS ONCE LOVED/SPRING

Word List

wishes	spring	second	either
wishbone	once	strongest	

I. Write a word from the Word List to match each definition.

1. heartiest ______________
2. something you desire ______________
3. meaning a choice can be made ______________
4. planting time ______________
5. next best; not first ______________

II. Complete the following sentences with a word from the Word List.

1. Whatever you have ______________ loved stays with you forever.
2. The speaker in the poem hopes that ______________ come true.
3. ______________ or summer is a good time to plant vegetables.
4. My sisters both want to win the pull of a ______________.
5. The ______________ person is able to lift the most weight.

III. On a separate sheet of paper, write a brief story using at least five words from the Word List. On the lines below, write the words that you used.

____

____

____

____

____

Name ______________________ Date ______________

WHAT IS ONCE LOVED/SPRING

Compare and Contrast

Two poems can be **compared** and **contrasted** by looking at how they are alike and how they are different. In "What Is Once Loved" the poet describes the memory of love. In "Spring" the poet describes a new love. We could compare the topics in each poem by saying they are both about love. We can contrast the topics in the poems by saying one is about past love and one is about a present love. Note how the comparison uses the word *both* and the contrast discusses what is unique to each poem.

Compare or contrast the following in the poems "What Is Once Loved" and "Spring."

1. Titles

COMPARISONS ______________________

____

CONTRASTS ______________________

____

2. Themes

COMPARISONS ______________________

____

CONTRASTS ______________________

____

3. Language

COMPARISONS ______________________

____

CONTRASTS ______________________

____

4. Audience

COMPARISONS ______________________

____

CONTRASTS ______________________

Name ______________________________ Date ______________

LUCKIEST TIME OF ALL *from* THE LUCKY STONE

Word List

plaited	**dogwood**	**throwing**	**twirled**
crokasack	**bottoms**	**pockets**	**gentle**
office	**excited**	**length**	**twine**
wonders	**gain**	**hero**	**acquainted**

I. Match each word in the left column with its definition in the right column.

1. twirled ____	**a.** progress; movement forward
2. gentle ____	**b.** tame; easy to handle
3. plaited ____	**c.** spun around in a circle
4. gain ____	**d.** how long something is
5. length ____	**e.** braided

II. Circle the letter of the word that best completes each sentence.

1. Sam needed something to use as a dog leash, so he cut a piece of ____ .

a. dogwood b. pockets c. twine

2. I was not ____ with a musician until I met you.

a. twirled b. acquainted c. plaited

3. They planted lowland crops in the ____, near the Mississippi River.

a. wonders b. length c. bottoms

4. Mark was so calm that he never got ____ about anything.

a. acquainted b. excited c. gentle

5. The pink and white blossoms on the ____ trees are beautiful in the spring.

a. dogwood b. crokasack c. office

Name ______________________________ *Date* ______________

LUCKIEST TIME OF ALL *from* THE LUCKY STONE

Identify the Author's Purpose

Before you even got to school today, you might have read parts of the newspaper, your cereal box, and a few billboards. Each of these examples has a purpose—usually to inform or persuade. Literature may also be written to *inform* or to *persuade,* as well as to *entertain* or *describe*. In fact, sometimes an author has several of these purposes in mind.

Read the following examples from "Luckiest Time of All," which was primarily written to entertain. Circle the letter of the choice below that best describes the author's purpose in addition to entertaining you.

1. "Usta be a kinda show went all through the South, called it the Silas Greene show. Somethin like the circus."

a. inform b. persuade c. describe

2. "Cutest one thing in the world next to you, Sweet Tee, dippin and movin and head bowin to that music. Had a little ruffly skirt on itself and up on two back legs twistin and movin to the music."

a. inform b. persuade c. describe

3. "That was the luckiest time of all, Tee Baby. It got me acquainted with Mr. Amos Pickens, and if that ain't luck, what could it be! Yes, it was luckier for me than for anybody, I think."

a. inform b. persuade c. describe

4. "He had a length of twine in his hand and he was twirlin it around in the air just like the cowboy at the Silas Greene and grinnin fit to bust."

a. inform b. persuade c. describe

Name ______________________________ Date ______________

STEPPING OUT WITH MY BABY

Word List

exhausting	**destination**	**automatically**	**technique**
severity	**hearty**	**demonstrating**	**illustrate**
ferocious	**fortunately**	**bifocals**	**corduroy**

I. Write the word from the Word List next to its correct definition below.

1. glasses for both near and far vision ____________
2. luckily ____________
3. very tiring ____________
4. a ribbed fabric ____________
5. showing how to do something ____________
6. the way something is done ____________

II. Circle the letter of the word from the Word List that best replaces each word in bold type.

1. We didn't realize the **seriousness** of the situation until the mudslide hit our house.

   a. destination b. severity c. technique

2. **Luckily**, we were not in it at the time, and were not injured.

   a. Fortunately b. Automatically c. Hearty

3. The moving wall of mud and rocks seemed almost like a **fierce** living thing.

   a. hearty b. exhausting c. ferocious

4. We were relieved when it reached its **ending point** before doing more damage.

   a. corduroy b. destination c. severity

5. There is no better way of **showing** the power of nature!

   a. demonstrating b. technique c. illustrate

Name ______________________________ Date ________________

STEPPING OUT WITH MY BABY

Distinguish Fact From Opinion

Nonfiction selections usually contain a combination of **facts** and **opinions**. To accurately evaluate what you read, you must be able to separate the facts from the opinions. Remember, facts can be measured or proven. Opinions are judgments that cannot be proven true or false.

Read the following sentences from "Stepping Out With My Baby." Write whether each sentence states a *fact*, an *opinion*, or *both*. Draw one line under each fact and two lines under each opinion found in the sentences.

1. Finally we arrive at the mailbox—an exhausting block and a half from home. ______________
2. What I seem to miss is the middle ground—the part where you share, teach, learn, play—the part you can actually enjoy. ______________
3. "So," I say to my buckled-up Beautiful Boy, "This is a mailbox." ______________
4. "The postal system was invented by Benjamin Franklin. In Philadelphia. He also invented bifocals." ______________
5. "See, this one goes to Aunt Ellen, who sent you that itchy sweater you hate. … " ______________
6. "What you want to do is: Pull down the handle, open the mailbox's mouth, and then you *flick* the letters in. You want to get that nice flicking motion in your wrist. … " ______________
7. My son smiles. I pull the handle up and down again. ______________
8. "What else can I tell you … the mailbox is blue." ______________
9. Talking to your baby is a lot like being on a first date: you feel like you're either saying too little or too much. ______________
10. As I buckle him back in, my son gives me one of those magnificent, otherworldly smiles. … ______________

Name ______________________ *Date* ______________

from THE TRAGEDY OF ROMEO AND JULIET

Word List

perverse	**prorogued**	**bescreened**	**purge**
nuptial	**peruse**	**profane**	**ward**
virtuous	**portly**	**rude**	**disparagement**
loathe	**prodigious**	**enmity**	**inexorable**
apprehend	**provoke**	**chide**	**unsavory**
detestable	**impeach**	**righteous**	**procure**
knave	**entreat**	**rapier**	**vengeance**

I. Complete each sentence with a word from the Word List.

1. Pamela decided to clean her room and ____________ all unused items.

2. Jamie is usually sneaky and dishonorable, but today he surprised us by being especially ____________ .

3. He looked forward to his trip to Europe and crossing the Atlantic to take ____________ on his enemies.

4. Building the pyramids in Egypt required ____________ effort.

5. I could never marry him—I ____________ that man!

II. Circle the letter of the word that best completes each sentence.

1. Sam did not mean to be impolite, but for some reason everyone thought he was ____ .

a. apprehend b. rude c. virtuous

2. He had planned to look at and ____ the books, but decided to go to the beach instead.

a. peruse b. entreat c. perverse

3. Although he was ____, he was not really considered fat.

a. unsavory b. righteous c. portly

Name ______________________________ *Date* ______________

from THE TRAGEDY OF ROMEO AND JULIET

Recognize Imagery

Writers use imagery to create pictures in the reader's mind. **Imagery** is the use of words that appeal to our senses of sight, smell, taste, hearing, and touch. For example, here is an excerpt from "Romeo and Juliet":

JULIET: … Sweet, good night!
This bud of love, by summer's ripening breath,
May prove a beautous flow'r when next we meet.

Shakespeare appeals to the reader's senses of smell and sight by using the image of a flower blooming in summer. This makes Juliet's growing love for Romeo vivid in the reader's mind.

Compare this use of imagery to the way the lines sound without imagery:

JULIET: The next time we meet our love will have grown.

Answer the questions about each of these excerpts from "Romeo and Juliet."

1. ROMEO: But soft! What light through yonder window breaks?
It is the East, and Juliet is the sun!
Arise, fair sun, and kill the envious moon.
Who is already sick and pale with grief
That thou her maid art far more fair than she.

What imagery is used to describe the moon? ______________________________

____

What senses are appealed to in this use of imagery? ______________________

____

2. JULIET: What's in a name? That which we call a rose
By any other word would smell as sweet.
So Romeo would, were he not Romeo called.

How is imagery used to explain that Romeo would be the same

even if his name were different? ______________________________

____

Which senses does the image appeal to?

____

Name ______________________ Date ______________

GREYDAY/HERE—HOLD MY HAND/FINIS

Word List

heavy	lonely	soul
eludes	resent	overmuch
empty	ache	finis

I. Circle the letter of the word that best completes each sentence.

1. The meaning of this poem ____ me; I don't understand it.

a. eludes b. lonely c. finis

2. If the ____ in your shoulder does not go away, you should see a doctor.

a. heavy b. woe c. ache

3. I like the painting because of its ____ feeling of deserted countryside.

a. overmuch b. lonely c. eludes

4. Once she gave the speech she felt ____ and had nothing left to say.

a. resent b. soul c. empty

5. Of all the people at the retreat, only one seemed to touch her ____ .

a. soul b. resent c. lonely

II. Write a word from the Word List to match each definition.

1. avoids ______________

2. central part of a person ______________

3. too great in amount ______________

4. end; conclusion ______________

5. massive ______________

Name ______________________ Date ______________

GREYDAY/HERE—HOLD MY HAND/FINIS

Paraphrase Poetry

To understand the meaning of a poem, you may find it helpful to **paraphrase**, or rewrite sections of the poem in your own words. If you aren't sure what a word or phrase means in a particular poem, read the other words around that word to get more information about the situation. Then you might be able to paraphrase a tricky phrase.

Read the following lines from the poems "Greyday," "Here—Hold My Hand," and "Finis." Write a paraphrase of each set of lines.

1. "The day hangs heavy/loose and grey/when you're away."

____

____

2. "A crown of thorns/a shirt of hair/is what I wear."

____

____

3. "there is/nothing/we can/ say ... your/soul eludes me"

____

____

4. " ... our love has drifted/to a quiet close,/Leaving the empty ache/
That always follows when beauty goes;"

____

____

5. "Go, dear, seek again the magic touch."

____

____

Name ______________________________ Date ______________

HOUSECLEANING/WHERE HAVE YOU GONE

Word List

dug	**habit**	**crooked**	**confident**
unfortunately	**departed**	**aware**	**rent**

I. Complete each sentence with a word from the Word List. Then look at the words below each sentence. Circle the letter of the antonym, or opposite, of the word you used to complete the sentence.

1. Craig was ____________ that his skills and experience would get him hired.

Antonym: a. daring b. insecure c. truthful

2. We all ____________ the White Lion concert and their music.

Antonym: a. attended b. hated c. liked

3. This is an incident that will ____________ damage our family business.

Antonym: a. luckily b. disastrously c. mournfully

II. Match each word from the left column with its correct definition from the right column.

1. dug ____ **a.** unluckily, inappropriately

2. unfortunately ____ **b.** gone away, left

3. confident ____ **c.** liked, enjoyed

4. habit ____ **d.** having faith, trust; showing assurance

5. departed ____ **e.** practice, custom

III. Write a brief story using at least five words from the Word List.

____

____

____

____

____

____

Name ______________________________ Date ______________

HOUSECLEANING/WHERE HAVE YOU GONE

Compare and Contrast

In both of these poems relationships are ending. Neither woman is particularly happy about the situation. However, the similarity ends there.

Answer the following questions.

i always liked housecleaning
even as a child
i dug straightening
the cabinets. …

1. What does the excerpt above tell you about the speaker? ______________________________

2. Why does the author compare housecleaning to ending a relationship? ______________________________

3. In "Where Have You Gone," who has ended the relationship? ______________________________

4. How does the writer feel about it? ______________________________

5. What does she mean when she says the sun went with him? ______________________________

6. These two poems show the writer in two very different positions, though in similar situations. What contrasting feelings do the women have? ______________________________

Name ______________________ Date ______________

WHERE ARE YOU NOW, WILLIAM SHAKESPEARE?

Word List

murky	correspondence	rivalry	deception
faze	journal	stroll	
rival	endure	venture	
reality	fiberboard	persist	

I. Write a word from the Word List to match each definition.

1. trick ____________

2. competition ____________

3. keep on going; say over and over ____________

4. risk; proceed onward ____________

5. walk leisurely ____________

II. Circle the letter of the word that best completes each sentence.

1. I did not want to ____ into the dark house alone, so I asked Tim to go with me.

a. persist b. rival c. venture

2. When Leanne tried to trip me before the cheerleading tryout, I knew that our ____ had gone too far.

a. correspondence b. rivalry c. reality

3. Although Enrico tried to sound sick when he called to say that he was not coming to work, no one was fooled by his ____.

a. rivalry b. venture c. deception

4. Even though I have cleaned it twice, this window still looks ____.

a. faze b. murky c. fiberboard

5. I think I will ____ down Main Street and look in the shop windows.

a. persist b. stroll c. endure

Name ______________________ Date ____________

WHERE ARE YOU NOW, WILLIAM SHAKESPEARE?

Analyze Details

Details make a story come alive. Authors provide details to create vivid descriptions, to drop clues in a mystery, make dialogue seem natural, and to simply make a story more interesting. Read the following excerpt from "Where Are You Now, William Shakespeare?" and note the underlined details.

> My very first boyfriend was named William Shakespeare. This was his real name, and he lived over on Highland Hill, about a block from my house.

The author used details to tell us a lot about the characters. If you analyzed—or put together—the underlined details, you might think that they may have met because they lived near each other.

Read the following excerpts from "Where Are You Now, William Shakespeare?" and underline the details you think are important. Then analyze what these details might mean in the story.

1. She was a tall redhead who looked like a girl, and who always had it in her head to fix meat loaf with mashed potatoes for a movie star named Spencer Tracy.

   ____

   ____

2. Dorothy Spencer was the first to hear from Ronald Reagan. She didn't get a letter, but she got a signed photograph.

   ____

   ____

3. By that time I had the photograph out. My heart began to beat nervously as I read the inscription at the bottom. "To a brave little girl, in admiration, Ronald Reagan."

   ____

   ____

Name ______________________ Date ______________

I DREAM A WORLD/REFLECTIONS

Word List

adorn	saps	blights	shame
scorn	avarice	wretchedness	
greed	bounties	sorrow	

I. Write a word from the Word List to match each definition.

1. embarrassment ______________
2. greed ______________
3. beautify ______________
4. disappoints ______________
5. snub ______________

II. Circle the letter of the word that best completes each sentence.

1. Etta wanted to ____ me with her mother's pearls.

   a. adorn b. scorn c. saps

2. I thought my ____ was under control, but I truly wished I could keep the pearls.

   a. sorrow b. shame c. avarice

3. Her ____ was easily exposed when the truth was told about the terrible things she had done.

   a. blights b. wretchedness c. saps

4. Her entire family shared her ____ when she lost her job.

   a. sorrow b. adorn c. avarice

5. She was likely to change how she felt by the typical ____ of early love: jealousy, pettiness, or disappointment.

   a. saps b. bounties c. blights

Name ______________________ Date ______________

I DREAM A WORLD/REFLECTIONS

Recognize Simile and Personification

A **simile** is a comparison of two things that are unrelated but have one trait in common. The words *like* or *as* are used in similes. **Personification** means to give human qualities to nonhuman objects. In the poem "I Dream A World" Langston Hughes uses both of these figures of speech:

Where wretchedness will hang its head,
And you, like a pearl,
Attends the needs of all mankind.

PERSONIFICATION: wretchedness will hang its head

INTERPRETATION: people will no longer be wretched

SIMILE: And you, like a pearl

INTERPRETATION: comparison of the pureness and beauty of a pearl to the people in the world (you).

Read each poem. Identify the use of personification and simile in each poem and interpret their meanings.

1. Love walks through our streets
Like a detective, searching for clues,
To solve this mystery we call life.
Will love find the answer?
Perhaps some day it will be the answer.

PERSONIFICATION: ______________________

INTERPRETATION: ______________________

SIMILE: ______________________

INTERPRETATION: ______________________

2. The world no longer cries in pain
Nor does it sing a sad refrain.
Like falling snow, the world today
Quietly falls and melts away.

PERSONIFICATION: ______________________

INTERPRETATION: ______________________

SIMILE: ______________________

INTERPRETATION: ______________________

Name ______________________________ *Date* ______________

APPOINTMENT IN BAGHDAD

Word List

assistant	appointment	Majesty	alarmed
Baghdad	Sultan	palace	astonished
escape	Damascus	skillful	

I. Write the word from the Word List that best matches each definition.

1. ruler of a Moslem country ______________
2. run away ______________
3. worried ______________
4. helper; aide ______________
5. place where royalty lives ______________
6. scheduled meeting ______________
7. surprised ______________
8. title used to address royalty ______________
9. capital of Syria ______________
10. capital of Iraq ______________

II. Circle the letter of the word that best completes each sentence.

1. George is a prompt person, so I expect him to be on time for the ________________ with the dentist.

   a. escape b. assistant c. appointment

2. When we flew into Iraq, the plane landed near the ______________ .

   a. Sultan b. Majesty c. palace

3. Dr. Pons is considered the most ______________ surgeon in the area.

   a. alarmed b. skillful c. assistant

4. We always referred to father as "Your ______________ ."

   a. Majesty b. assistant c. Sultan

5. The Sultan was ______________ at the wondrous speed of the horse.

   a. skillful b. alarmed c. astonished

Name ______________________________ Date ______________

APPOINTMENT IN BAGHDAD

Draw Conclusions

A **conclusion** is an inference based on evidence. When you read, you can use evidence in the story to draw conclusions about characters' actions and attitudes.

Read each paragraph and answer the question that follows.

1. Elyse once swore she would never enter the attic of her home. It was probably creepy and full of cobwebs. Yet, the weeping and shuddering sighs which came from behind the attic drew her to the old oak attic door. Without a thought she yanked it open.

What can you conclude about Elyse's personality? ______________________________

____

____

2. John rarely took the lakeside road. It was shorter, true, but the road was also dimly lit and wound upon itself like a snake. The main road was safer, but it made a big loop around the woods. But with only ten minutes left to spare, he took the dangerous lakeside road.

What can you conclude about the reason for John's decision? ______________________

____

____

3. The coach had warned Paula that she was missing too many basketball practices. The other day she was late for a game. The coach didn't say anything at the time, but the next day, Paula's teacher handed her a note from the coach.

What can you conclude about the contents of the note? ______________________

____

____

Name ______________________________ *Date* ______________

APPOINTMENT AT NOON/ INCIDENT IN A ROSE GARDEN

Word List

apologetic	**scowl**	**sincerity**	**dimensionless**
mouthpiece	**somber**	**precognition**	**scythe**

I. Complete each sentence with a word from the Word List.

1. She had a ______________ that he would bring her candy that day.

2. With a ______________ expression he told us of our father's death.

3. When we arrested the thief he told us he wanted to call his ______________ .

4. We could never doubt his ______________ as honest as he was.

5. Time had a ______________ quality to it; it seemed to stand still.

II. Write the letter of the word that best defines how each italicized word is used in the sentence.

____ **1.** He was very *apologetic* about being late.

a. angry b. sorry c. annoyed

____ **2.** The *scowl* on his face made us wary of him.

a. angry look b. grin c. questioning look

____ **3.** His air of *sincerity* made us inclined to believe him.

a. happiness b. charm c. honesty

____ **4.** He used a *scythe* to cut the grass.

a. mower b. curved blade c. hedge trimmer

____ **5.** The ride on the roller coaster made time and space *dimensionless.*

a. indescribable b. boundless c. limited

Name ______________________ Date ______________

Appointment At Noon/ Incident in a Rose Garden

Make Inferences

Sometimes an author will state directly the relationship between two characters:

> Mark and Jean were friends for twenty years.

Sometimes you must figure out the relationship between characters based on the clues the author provides:

> Although they were not family, Mark was always there for Jean. For twenty years Jean knew that if she needed help, or just wanted to talk to someone, Mark was there. And Mark knew the same about Jean.

From the clues "they were not family," "always there," "if she needed help … Mark was there," and "Mark knew the same about Jean," you can infer that Mark and Jean are close friends who have known each other for a long time.

Read the excerpt from the story, "Appointment At Noon," and answer the questions.

> "What's wrong with you?" he snapped when Miss Reed came in. "You get worse every day. Old age creeping over you or something?"
>
> She paused. She was tall, neat, and steady. She faced him across the desk, her eyes showing a touch of fear. Curran hired to work for him only people he knew too much about.

1. What kind of relationship does Curran have with Miss Reed? ______________________

____

2. What clues lead you to infer this relationship? ______________________

____

3. What kind of relationship does Miss Reed have with Curran? ______________________

____

4. What clues lead you to infer this relationship? ______________________

____

Name ______________________ Date ____________

BOY IN THE SHADOWS

Word List

ition	disquieting
ies	mirthlessly
d	scraggy
	pneumonia
y	

write the letter of the correct

iches of hairs or grass

ling of fear or horror

shes or small trees growing close
ether

ne with effort

n and worn from worry

s each sentence.

re the ____.

ps

ft

n Texas in which the
through.

icket

4. Children around the world who do not get proper food can die from ____.

a. malnutrition b. authorities c. pneumonia

5. He was known to ____ tease his brothers.

a. slackly b. listlessly c. mirthlessly

Name ______________________________ *Date* ______________

BOY IN THE SHADOWS

Make Predictions

In the story, "Boy in the Shadows," the author provides clues for the reader to **make predictions** about the ending. For example, read this excerpt:

> Is it true that love is stronger than death? That the human spirit can survive the grave?

It is evident from these opening lines that this story is going to deal in some way with love and death. This is the reader's first clue to predicting the outcome of the story.

Read each excerpt and answer the questions.

1. His mother beckoned Irene to one side and spoke in a low voice. " … When I come, you can give me his two dollars."

"But what about Jayse?" Irene asked. "If he's working for the money, shouldn't I pay it to him?"

Would it be a reasonable prediction that Irene is going to become involved in Jayse's mother's business? Why or why not?

____

____

2. Ernest got up and came to stand at her side. "I could have told you that. He always sits there at night. As far as I know, he never sleeps. I'll admit he's one spooky kid—but he's not bothering anyone, is he?"

No one but me, Irene thought. As the days wore on, the sight of the boy wrung her heart. His skin, which had been pale, was now yellow and shiny. There were discolored patches on his forehead, cheekbones, and along the ridge of his nose.

From this excerpt could you predict that Jayse is very unusual and not just a quiet worker? Why or why not?

____

____

Name ______________________________ Date ______________

SORRY, WRONG NUMBER

Word List

self-centered	**client**	**unspeakably**	**apprehend**
explicitly	**specific**	**invalid**	**drastic**
red tape	**precinct**	**stark**	**inefficient**
coincidence	**vague**	**exclusive**	**registry**
fiendish	**entitled**	**unnerved**	
catechizing	**civic**	**cold-blooded fiends**	

I. Write the word from the Word List that matches each synonym.

1. catch ______________
2. restricted ______________
3. inept ______________
4. inexpressible ______________
5. permitted ______________

II. Circle the letter of the word that best completes each sentence.

1. Mrs. Stevenson thought only of herself. She was ____ .

   a. vague b. self-centered c. specific

2. Mark is always misplacing things and forgetting to complete tasks. He is very ____ .

   a. invalid b. drastic c. inefficient

3. His birthday and mine are on the same day. What a ____ .

   a. stark b. coincidence c. entitled

4. She understood that the teacher did not give clear and ____ instructions, which made it difficult to understand assignments.

   a. specific b. invalid c. client

5. The evidence was ____ and was not enough to convict the accused man of robbery.

   a. vague b. specific c. drastic

Name ______________________________ Date ______________

SORRY, WRONG NUMBER

Make Inferences From Conversation

In the play, "Sorry, Wrong Number," the reader learns about the characters, plot, and setting through a telephone conversation. Sometimes an author gives only one side of a conversation and the reader must infer what is being said by someone else. For example:

> "Of course I do, but unfortunately I can't go out, even if it is only for a quick bite."

The clue, "even if it is only for a quick bite," allows the reader to infer that the person has just been asked out to eat.

First, read the conversation, then on the lines *above* each quote, write what you think might have been said.

1. Larry: ______________________________

____

Peter: I'm sorry to hear that, Larry. But the fact is that you still owe me $500. After all, I did my job and I expect to get paid for it.

2. Secretary: ______________________________

____

Boss: Just keep trying. I know he's there. I just dropped him off and he said he was going to do some work. He's bound to answer sooner or later.

3. Doctor: ______________________________

____

Patient: I don't know. I suppose it started last week and sort of came and went during the day. But it's the nights that are the worst. My head feels like it's going to explode at night.

4. Marge: ______________________________

____

Jill: I've heard that before. Last month you joined a health club and went only two times. And you still have a closet full of powdered diet food that could last you six months.

Name ______________________________ *Date* ________________

THUS I REFUTE BEELZY

Word List

scullery	**mechanism**	**anatomy**	**fantasy**
obstinate	**perverse**	**morsel**	
gesticulating	**civil**	**ritual**	

I. Match the words in the left column with their correct definitions in the right column.

1. scullery ____	**a.** polite
2. obstinate ____	**b.** body
3. fantasy ____	**c.** improper
4. ritual ____	**d.** room next to the kitchen
5. perverse ____	**e.** system like a machine
6. morsel ____	**f.** stubborn
7. civil ____	**g.** using hands to motion
8. mechanism ____	**h.** something imagined
9. anatomy ____	**i.** small piece
10. gesticulating ____	**j.** a set pattern

II. Circle the letter of the word that best completes each sentence.

1. We knew that Father was too ____ to change his mind.
a. civil   b. obstinate   c. gesticulating

2. After such a big argument, it was all David and his neighbor could do to be ____ to each other.
a. civil   b. perverse   c. obstinate

3. Your idea about being the most popular person at school is nothing but a ____ .
a. ritual   b. morsel   c. fantasy

4. Since I am on a diet, I will have only a ____ of cake.
a. scullery   b. morsel   c. mechanism

5. The ____ on the printer that moved the paper was broken.
a. scullery   b. mechanism   c. anatomy

Name ______________________ Date ______________

THUS I REFUTE BEELZY

Analyze Characters' Responses

Use both the information in the story and your own experience to **analyze characters' responses**. Characters are the people, and sometimes animals, in the story. Authors often provide clues about characters in their response to events or other characters. For example, read this excerpt from "Thus I Refute Beelzy."

> "Small Simon, you are being obstinate," said Mr. Carter ... The little boy looked down at his plate, smiling resignedly.

The little boy smiles resignedly in response to being called obstinate. You can infer that he accepts the fact that his father thinks he is obstinate.

Read the excerpts below. Analyze the characters' responses to each other.

1. "I hope you are listening to me," said his father, "All you have to do is say, 'I have been playing a game of let's pretend ... Mr. Beelzy is a daydream.'"

The little boy still stared at his plate.

ANALYZE SON'S RESPONSE: ______________________

____

2. "He is sometimes there and sometimes not there," pursued Mr. Carter. "Sometimes he's like one thing, sometimes another. You can't really see him ... " Mr. Carter stretched out his big, white, dentist's hand, and took his little son by the shoulder. He stopped speaking for a moment and tightened his hand.

ANALYZE FATHER'S RESPONSE: ______________________

____

3. The little boy sank his head still lower.

"I hope you are listening to me."

ANALYZE SON'S RESPONSE: ______________________

____

Name ______________________ Date ______________

HIST, WHIST/OVERHEARD ON A SALTMARSH

Word List

scuttling	**nymph**	**tweeds**
lagoon	**howl**	**goblin**

I. Write the word from the Word List that best matches each definition.

1. nature goddess in Greek or Roman mythology ______________

2. moving quickly ______________

3. shallow body of water connected to a larger one ______________

4. loud, wailing cry ______________

5. type of weave on a man's suit ______________

II. Circle the letter of the word that best completes each sentence.

1. We could tell that a storm was coming up because the birds were ____ about the yard for food.

a. scuttling b. tweeds c. howl

2. Mortimer had a dream in which he went fishing in the ____.

a. howl b. nymph c. lagoon

3. Ted dressed in ____ making him look like a typical college professor.

a. tweeds b. howl c. lagoon

4. The story was about a mischievous ____ who lived in the woods and played tricks on hunters.

a. scuttling b. nymph c. lagoon

5. Her nightmares were filled with ghosts and ____.

a. nymph b. goblins c. tweeds

Name ______________________ *Date* ______________

HIST, WHIST/OVERHEARD ON A SALTMARSH

Identify Mood

Mood is a feeling an author is trying to convey. It can be humorous, scary, playful, or sad. It is up to the reader to infer the mood of a story from the words the author uses. What mood can you infer from these lines of "hist, whist"?

hist   whist
little ghostthings
tip-toe
twinkle-toe

Although the subject of ghosts is often scary and mysterious, here the words "little ghostthings" and "twinkle-toe" give a light-hearted feeling to the poem. The mood could be described as light-hearted, gleeful, or playful.

Read these excerpts, describe each mood, and write the words that determined the mood.

1. little hoppy happy/toad in the tweeds

MOOD: ______________________

WORDS THAT DETERMINE THE MOOD: ______________________

2. I will howl in a deep lagoon/For your green glass beads, I love them so …

MOOD: ______________________

WORDS THAT DETERMINE THE MOOD: ______________________

3. "I have said you must be allowed to learn from experience. Go upstairs. Right up to your room. You shall learn whether it is better to reason, or to be perverse and obstinate. Go up."

MOOD: ______________________

WORDS THAT DETERMINE THE MOOD: ______________________

4. "You've got to hear me. Oh, please, you've got to help me. There's someone in this house. Someone who's going to murder me."

MOOD: ______________________

WORDS THAT DETERMINE THE MOOD: ______________________

Name ______________________ Date ______________

The Judge's House

Word List

absurd	**bogies**	**coincidence**	**deliberately**
evade	**gables**	**malignant**	**relic**
rigid	**tremor**	**wainscot**	

I. Write the letter of the correct definition of each numbered word.

1. rigid ____
2. bogies ____
3. coincidence ____
4. wainscot ____
5. gables ____
6. deliberately ____
7. tremor ____
8. absurd ____
9. evade ____
10. malignant ____

a. in an unhurried manner
b. a seemingly remarkable chance occurrence of two things at the same time
c. a facing for the walls in a room
d. a quick, vibrating movement; shaking
e. the triangular top parts of an outer wall, between the sides of a sloped roof
f. things that startle or frighten
g. avoid
h. ridiculous
i. evil
j. stiff

II. Use a word from the Word List that best completes each sentence.

1. Michelle did not know the answer. She tried to ______________ the question.
2. Josh is afraid to be alone in his room at night. He thinks ______________ live under his bed.
3. In the attic I found an old ______________ from the Civil War.
4. Marco's ideas about how to make money are silly and ______________. He wants to sell the garbage of famous people as art.
5. Marisa took her time and strolled ______________ to her friend's house.

Name ______________________________ *Date* ______________

THE LISTENERS/ELDORADO

Draw Conclusions

Sometimes you must use the details of a selection or poem and your own experience to figure out an unstated event, or action. What conclusion can you draw about the knight from this excerpt of the poem, "Eldorado"?

And o'er his heart a shadow
Fell as he found no spot of ground
That looked like Eldorado.

Although the poet does not directly state it, the line "And o'er his heart a shadow" tells the reader that the knight is sad and discouraged because, as yet, he has not found Eldorado.

Read these lines from the poem, "The Listeners" and answer the questions.

But only a host of phantom listeners
That dwelt in the lone house then
Stood listening in the quiet of the moonlight
To that voice from the world of men:

1. What conclusion can you draw about who the listeners are?

____

2. Which clues led you to this conclusion and why?

____

____

3. What time of the day does this poem take place?

____

4. Which clues led you to this conclusion and why?

____

____

Ay, they heard his foot upon the stirrup,
And the sound of iron on stone,

5. What is making the sound of iron on stone?

____

6. What clues led you to this conclusion and why?

____

from Pieces of the Frame*

Word List

transmitter	telephoto	crossbow	slug
glens	amphibious	ad infinitum	Gaelic
newt	genus	Parliament	basking
fortnight	incantations	technique	reconnaissance
caravans	fanatical	perfunctory	

I. Write the word from the Word List that best fits each definition.

1. narrow, secluded valleys ______________
2. radio device that sends signals ______________
3. warming oneself in sunlight ______________
4. a two week time period ______________
5. words that are chanted to cast a spell ______________
6. a group of closely related species ______________
7. able to live on land and in water ______________
8. routine; superficial ______________
9. method of doing something ______________
10. small salamander found in damp places ______________

II. Complete the following sentences with a word from the Word List.

1. A ______________ lens works like a pair of binoculars.
2. The legislative body in Great Britain is called ______________.
3. Once he starts speaking on his favorite subject he will speak ______________.
4. If a snail doesn't have a shell, you call it a ______________.
5. After making a ______________ of the enemy's position, we found we were in greater danger than we had previously believed.

**May have been titled "The Lock Ness Monster" in previous printings.*

from PIECES OF THE FRAME*

Evaluate the Writer's Purpose

Writers can entertain, persuade, inform, and express their feelings in their writing. Often a writer uses a combination of these purposes. As a reader, **evaluate the writer's purpose** or purposes by asking yourself these questions:

1. Is the writer trying to entertain me by making me laugh or smile?
2. Is the writer trying to persuade me to believe or do something?
3. Is the writer informing me by giving me facts and information?
4. Is the writer expressing his or her own feelings through a story or poem?

Once you have determined the purpose, or purposes, ask yourself whether the writer was effective in entertaining, persuading, informing, or expressing feelings.

Read each of these excerpts and state the main purpose the writer had in mind and whether it was effective.

1. "Gulls are inland birds in Scotland, there being so little distance from anywhere to the sea."

PURPOSE: ______________________________

WHY IS THIS EFFECTIVE? ______________________________

____

2. "Probably the one word that might have been applied to everyone present was adventurer."

PURPOSE: ______________________________

WHY IS THIS EFFECTIVE? ______________________________

____

3. "It is *not* poisonous. Leave it alone. Look at all these children."

PURPOSE: ______________________________

WHY IS THIS EFFECTIVE? ______________________________

____

**May have been titled "The Lock Ness Monster" in previous printings.*

Name ______________________________ Date ______________

The Great Amherst Mystery

Word List

poltergeist	**deception**	**vocation**
avocation	**demonstration**	**wonderful**

I. Match each word from the left column by writing the letter of its correct definition from the right column.

1. wonderful ____ **a.** a noisy ghost

2. vocation ____ **b.** happening that can be observed

3. deception ____ **c.** profession; career

4. poltergeist ____ **d.** curious; strange

5. demonstration ____ **e.** trickery

6. avocation ____ **f.** hobby

II. Circle the letter of the word that best completes each sentence.

1. Sergio was interested in a career or ____ working with computers.

a. poltergeist b. vocation c. demonstration

2. Mona knew that trickery was one of Jon's techniques to attract girls, so she was not fooled by his ____ .

a. wonderful b. avocation c. deception

3. She had never received such a strange, ____ gift.

a. wonderful b. deception c. poltergeist

4. The science teacher ended the class with a ____ of a chemical reaction.

a. avocation b. vocation c. demonstration

5. To get away from his job in the city, Bob retreats to his country house, where he enjoys his favorite ____ of butterfly collecting.

a. poltergeist b. avocation c. vocation

Name ______________________ Date ______________

The Great Amherst Mystery

Make Inferences About Setting

In "The Great Amherst Mystery," the author directly states that the action takes place "in a big old house in the town of Amherst." However, sometimes the reader must infer where a story takes place by using clues the writer provides. For example, where does the following excerpt take place?

> I used to meet Ralph every Saturday morning in front of his apartment building. We'd go across the street and play ball in the empty lot. Then we'd run down the block to Nick's Candy Store for a tall, cool soda.

You can infer that this takes place in a city because of the apartment building, empty lot, and candy store.

Below are revisions of the previous excerpt which include clues that change the setting of the story. Read each, then identify the clues and tell where the new version takes place.

1. I used to go to his house to get him, or I'd meet him near the red barn at Mr. Watson's place, or over at the cornfield. There we would play hide and seek when the corn was high and just have foot races when it wasn't.

CLUES: ______________________

SETTING: ______________________

2. I used to meet Ralph at his condominium, or near the boat docks at Watson's Yacht Club, or over at the private beach club. There we would play tennis or just sun ourselves by the olympic-sized pool we enjoyed so much in those days.

CLUES: ______________________

____

SETTING: ______________________

3. I used to meet Ralph near the water fountain right before the first bell. Then we'd go to our lockers, get the books we needed, and see who Nancy Quin would say hello to first, when we both walked into class.

CLUES: ______________________

SETTING: ______________________

Name ______________________ *Date* ______________

THE GETAWAY

Word List

root	**feed merchant**	**El Paso**
Rio Grande	**Chihuahua**	**Juárez**

I. Choose a word from the Word List to match each definition.

1. person who buys and sells food for animals ______________
2. city in Western Texas, near the Mexican border ______________
3. dig around or search ______________
4. Mexican city across the river from El Paso ______________
5. river that separates Texas from Mexico ______________
6. city in northern Mexico ______________

II. Choose the word from the Word List that best completes each sentence.

1. The men hoped to find a bridge across the ______________.
2. On our trip to Mexico, we visited ______________, a city across the river from the El Paso.
3. I had to ______________ around in the attic to find my old cheer-leading uniform.
4. ______________ is the name of a Mexican city, and it is also a breed of dog.
5. The ______________ delivered several bushels of grain for our cow.

Name ______________________ Date ______________

SHERLOCK HOLMES AND THE SPECKLED BAND

Evaluate the Writer's Craft

Writers use many techniques to tell their stories. For example, a writer may want the reader to understand a character's personality trait. The writer may offer an event as a way to lead the reader to understand a character. For example, read this excerpt from the play, "Sherlock Holmes and the Speckled Band":

> HOLMES: Now ... what sent you all this way by train? And so early in the morning, too.
> HELEN: How did you know I ... ?
> HOLMES: There's the second half of a return ticket in the palm of your left glove. Plain as day ...

Notice how the author shows how observant Holmes is by having him notice a ticket in a glove.

Read these excerpts. Use the list below to choose the writer's main purpose and describe the technique the writer used to accomplish it.

WRITER'S PURPOSE LIST
create suspense
indirectly describe a character
explain the solution to a mystery

1. HELEN: She was twisting in terrible pain. I bent over her. Then suddenly she shrieked—I'll never forget her voice! "Oh Helen! It was the band! The speckled band!"
   HOLMES: That's all? She didn't explain?

   ____

   ____

2. ROYLOTT: I'll go when I've had my say. Don't *dare* meddle with my business. I know she's been here. I traced her! I'm a dangerous man to go up against!

   ____

   ____

3. WATSON: But who'd think of a snake?
   HOLMES: I thought of it right away. Remember, the doctor had pets from India. We knew that. A snake seemed just the sort of weapon he'd choose. ...

   ____

   ____

Name ______________________ Date ______________

TRIFLES

Word List

attorney	wiry	pneumonia	twitches
notified	strangled	expose	instinct
shabby	abruptly	crafty	sarcastic
quilt	abashed	fidgety	apologetically
covert	peering	snatches	pleasantries
preoccupied	scoffingly	supervising	superstitious
facetiously	trifles	gallantry	preserves

I. Match each word from the left column by writing the letter of its correct definition from the right column.

1. peering ____
2. scoffingly ____
3. facetiously ____
4. quilt ____
5. pneumonia ____

a. disease of the lungs
b. looking closely
c. a bed cover
d. spoken with scorn
e. jokingly, especially at an inappropriate time

II. Circle the letter of the word that best completes each sentence.

1. His mother seemed ____. He knew she was thinking of something else, although she tried to appear as if she were listening.

   a. facetiously b. preoccupied c. expose

2. Jean Luc was embarrassed and ____ when Marie told him how much she cared for him.

   a. wiry b. abashed c. covert

3. The beggar was poorly dressed and appeared ____ compared to the well-dressed people leaving the concert.

   a. shabby b. pleasantries c. preoccupied

4. We hired an ____ to help us with our court case.

   a. abashed b. abruptly c. attorney

5. His ____ activities were not noticed by anyone.

   a. covert b. instinct c. strangled

Name ______________________________ *Date* ______________

TRIFLES

Draw Conclusions

Draw conclusions by applying what you know about people and situations to the characters and events in a story. Often a writer reveals a character or event through dialogue and you know that there is sometimes hidden meaning in what people say. For example, here is one character speaking in the play, "Trifles":

> SHERIFF: Well, can you beat women. Held for murder and worrying about her preserves.

You can draw the conclusion that the sheriff is having trouble understanding why the woman is not more worried about being in jail.

Read each excerpt and draw a conclusion about each character's statement.

1. MRS. PETERS: She said she wanted an apron. Funny thing to want for there isn't much to get you dirty in jail, goodness knows. But I suppose just to make her feel more natural.

YOUR CONCLUSION: ______________________________

____

2. MRS. HALE: I might have known she needed help. I know how things can be—for women. I tell you it's queer, Mrs. Peters. We live close together and we live far apart.

YOUR CONCLUSION: ______________________________

____

3. MRS. PETERS: … My, it's a good thing the men couldn't hear us. Wouldn't they just laugh! Getting all stirred up over a little thing like a—dead canary. As if that could have anything to do with—with—wouldn't they laugh!

YOUR CONCLUSION: ______________________________

____

Name ______________________ Date ______________

THE RATTLESNAKE HUNT *from* CROSS CREEK

Word List

everglade	**coupe**	**portable**	**herpetologist**
meshed	**data**	**varmints**	**desolate**
cypress	**gopher**	**companion**	**jolting**
prong	**vegetation**	**sluggish**	**crocus sack**
buttonwood	**attitude**	**saffron**	**paralyzing**
aggressors	**hummocks**	**blunt**	**resent**

I. Circle the letter of the word that best completes each sentence.

1. Few trees grow in water like the ____, a species of tree found in the swamps of the South.

a. everglade b. varmints c. cypress

2. An ____ is a large swampland covered with tall grass.

a. everglade b. buttonwood c. saffron

3. The radio that Rex took with him to the ballgames was easy to carry because it was ____.

a. desolate b. portable c. meshed

4. It was hardly a mountain range, just a row of grassy ____.

a. hummocks b. varmints c. aggressors

5. They were always together, to each a ____ for life.

a. saffron b. gopher c. companion

II. Complete the following sentences with a word from the Word List.

1. David carried a metal pole with a ____ end.

2. The scientists used facts and ____ about the birth and death of stars to project the Big Bang theory.

3. The venom of some snakes has a ____ effect, leaving the victim unable to move.

4. While a botanist is a scientist who studies plants, a ____ is a scientist who studies reptiles and amphibians.

5. A special court was set up to punish the ____.

Name ______________________ Date ______________

THE RATTLESNAKE HUNT *from* CROSS CREEK

Identify Problems and Solutions

The plot of a story often revolves around a **problem.** A problem is often introduced for one or more of the characters, who then spend the rest of the story trying to find a **solution** to the problem. For example, in "The Rattlesnake Hunt" the main problem is that the author is afraid of snakes. She solves the problem by going on a rattlesnake hunt with a young herpetologist.

Read the following problems. Then write a plausible solution to the problem.

1. A boy is worried that he won't pass a history test.

SOLUTION: ______________________

____

2. A woman wants to learn how to play the piano but she doesn't have enough money for lessons.

SOLUTION: ______________________

____

3. A river is overflowing its banks because of heavy rains.

SOLUTION: ______________________

____

4. A zoo has to figure out what to do with a favorite monkey when they close the zoo next year.

SOLUTION: ______________________

____

5. A girl has to figure out how to get her cat out of a tall tree.

SOLUTION: ______________________

____

Name ______________________________ Date ______________

EARTH/EARTH

Word List

cockroaches	**Martian**	**lice**
maggots	**shrivelling**	

I. Write the word from the Word List that matches each definition.

1. small wormlike animals that are the young form of flies or other insects ______________
2. shrinking; drying up ______________
3. inhabitant of Mars ______________
4. large black or brown insects that live in buildings, especially old or dirty buildings ______________
5. small insects that can live in the skin and hair of people. ______________

II. Complete the following sentences with a word from the Word List.

1. Do you believe there are ______________ living on Mars?
2. We found that the apples on our tree were being eaten by ______________, which are young forms of flies.
3. The children were checked by the school nurse to see if they had ______________ in their hair.
4. Without water, the young plants began ______________.
5. Big brown insects like beetles and ______________ give me the creeps!

III. Write a paragraph in which you use each of the words in the Word List.

____

____

____

____

____

____

Name ______________________ Date ____________

EARTH/EARTH

Evaluate the Author's Style

Style, which is the manner in which an author makes a point, is sometimes as important as the point being made. In his poem, "Earth," John Wheelock used a Martian to tell the reader about the Earth's explosion. He also used rhyme. Do you think the poem would have had the same impact if he didn't use this style?

Read the lines from Herford's poem, "Earth." Then tell whether each evaluation of style is true or false. Explain your answers.

If this little world tonight
  Suddenly should fall through space
In a hissing headlong flight,
  Shrivelling from off its face,
As it falls into the sun,
  In an instant every trace
Of little crawling things—
  Ants, philosophers, and lice,
Cattle, cockroaches, and kings,
  Beggars, millionaires, and mice,
Men and maggots all as one
  As it falls into the sun. ...

1. The poet uses rhyme to make the poem sound almost lyrical.

   True or False? ______________________

   ____

2. The use of alliteration (two or more words in a row with the same beginning sounds) adds to the poetic sound of the words.

   True or False? ______________________

   ____

3. The use of similes (comparing the quality of one unlike thing to another using the words *like* or *as*) throughout the poem makes the images more clear.

   True or False? ______________________

   ____

Name ______________________________ *Date* ______________

THE LADY OR THE TIGER?

Word List

genial	reflect	station	fair
subject	semi-barbaric	portals	relentless
tribunal	doleful	fancies	perception

I. Alphabetize the words in the Word List. The first word is done for you.

1. doleful
2. ____________
3. ____________
4. ____________
5. ____________
6. ____________
7. ____________
8. ____________
9. ____________
10. ____________
11. ____________
12. ____________

I. Circle the letter of the word that best completes each sentence.

1. Jack thought that he deserved a better place in life—a ____ among the rich and famous.

   a. subject b. tribunal c. station

2. As the child grew older its awareness and ____ grew.

   a. perception b. fair c. genial

3. Some experts think that babies are uncivilized and ____ until they learn to communicate.

   a. portals b. doleful c. semi-barbaric

4. Mikyung wanted to think about the problem in depth, to have more time to ____ before having to answer.

   a. subject b. doleful c. reflect

5. Mr. Albright had a ____ disposition and an appealing laugh.

   a. doleful b. genial c. fancies

6. Everyone thought the queen was ____. They admired her beauty.

   a. reflect b. tribunal c. fair

Name ______________________________ Date ______________

THE LADY OR THE TIGER?

Make Judgments

When you judge a selection, you can base your evaluation on several aspects of the work: the characters, the setting, the style, the plot, or the ending. The opinions given in an evaluation should be based on information directly contained in the selection. Here is an evaluation of the story, "The Lady or the Tiger?"

> This story kept my interest right from the beginning. The description of the unusual punishment this king had set up for criminals was very entertaining. The king was the best character in the story. His all-consuming love of power was very amusing. The fast-moving plot filled me with suspense right up to the end. However, I did not like the ending. I think a story should have a definite way of ending. I believe that the author shows a bit of weakness by leaving it up to the reader to decide on an ending.

I. Answer these questions about the preceding evaluation.

1. Did the writer of the evaluation like the story? ______________________

   How was this opinion supported? ______________________

   ____

2. Did the writer evaluate the characters? ______________________

   What was this opinion and how was it supported? ______________________

   ____

3. What evaluation was made about the ending? ______________________

   ____

4. How was this opinion supported? ______________________

   ____

II. Now it's your turn. On the lines below, write an evaluation of the story, "The Lady or the Tiger?" Include other story elements that were not mentioned in the preceding evaluation, such as setting, other characters, and style. You may also include some of the elements that were mentioned—in particular, the ending.

____

____

____

____

Name ______________________________ *Date* ______________

DISPLAYS OF SKILL: THE BAT/ THE BIRD OF NIGHT

Word List

mammal	**flight-borne**	**heaves**	**swells**
nourishment	**swift**	**deploy**	**eaves**

I. Write the word from the Word List that matches each definition.

1. lifts up with effort ______________

2. lower edges of a roof ______________

3. increases in size, volume, or force ______________

4. food ______________

5. able to fly ______________

6. a member of the highest class of vertebrate animals ______________

7. spread out systematically ______________

8. a bird capable of extreme speed ______________

II. Complete the following sentences with words from the Word List.

1. A bat has an advantage over other animals because it is ______________ .

2. The ______________ bird was able to move faster than the others.

3. The General decided to ______________ troops to the area on the other side of the river.

4. The birds made nests under the ______________ of the house.

5. The squirrel came into the picnic area hoping to find some ______________ .

Name ______________________ *Date* ____________

Displays of Skill: The Bat/ The Bird of Night

Evaluate Facts

The poem "Displays of Skill: The Bat" contains facts about bats. Of course, the facts are written as poetry, but the author had to find the facts before writing the poem. But after looking up the facts, the author may then choose to exaggerate or add fanciful ideas. When you read a poem, think about the statements in it. Which do you think are facts and which are fancies?

Read the following lines from "Displays of Skill: The Bat" and answer the questions that follow.

Sleep, sleep is my nourishment, I sleep
All day, all winter, and my young's but one.
At first I fly with it at my breast, even hunting,
But if it bores me I hang it on a wall
And go it alone, enjoying insects frankly.
Tons, tons, I devour tons of insects, half
Of my weight is insects eaten within one night,

1. Animals that sleep through the winter are said to hibernate. Do you think that bats hibernate? What statements in the poem support your answer?

____

____

2. Reread the fourth line above. Do you think a bat gets bored? Do you think a bat could hang its baby on a wall?

____

____

3. Reread the last two lines above. How much of that information do you think is accurate?

____

____

Name ______________________________ Date ______________

A SECRET FOR TWO

Word List

Montreal	**gout**	**pension**
sheen	**cobbled**	**peak**
stalk	**Monsieur**	**cataract**

I. Complete these sentences with words from the Word List.

1. To relieve the discomfort of his ____________ he propped his foot up on the television set.
2. The aging Mr. Wong was losing sight in his left eye because a ____________ was beginning to form.
3. Before streets were paved with asphalt or with brick, they were ____________.
4. Melinda's red hair has a radiant color and ____________ that is very unusual.
5. One of the benefits of working with some companies is that you may qualify for retirement pay, or a ____________.
6. The woman's pride and anger caused her to ____________ away.
7. He lowered the ____________ of his cap to keep the sun out of his eyes.
8. She had always wanted to live in a Canadian city, such as ____________.

II. Match each word from the left column by writing the letter of its correct definition from the right column.

1. Monsieur ____
2. peak ____
3. gout ____
4. pension ____
5. cobbled ____

a. painful joint disease
b. retirement plan
c. French word for *Mister*
d. front part of a cap
e. paved with rounded stones

Name ______________________________ *Date* ______________

A SECRET FOR TWO

Make Inferences

As you read you **make inferences**—think about what the facts you are reading actually mean—to help you understand a selection. Read this excerpt from "A Secret for Two."

> "I couldn't help it," the driver of the truck protested. "He walked right into my truck. He never saw it, I guess. Why, he walked into it as though he were blind."

You can infer from the dialogue how confused the driver was about why the horse hit his truck. You can also infer that he is concerned that he might be blamed for the accident.

Read the following excerpts. For each excerpt, make an inference about what the information means in the story.

1. Montreal is a very large city, but, like all large cities, it has some very small streets. Streets, for instance, like Prince Edward Street, which is only four blocks long.

INFERENCE ABOUT MONTREAL: ______________________________

____

____

2. "This is a kind horse, a gentle and faithful horse," Pierre said. "I can see a beautiful spirit shining out of the eyes of the horse. I will name him after good St. Joseph, who was also kind and gentle and faithful and a beautiful saint."

INFERENCE ABOUT PIERRE: ______________________________

____

____

3. So it went on for years—always the same. Pierre and Joseph both grew old together, but gradually, not suddenly. Pierre's walrus mustache was pure white now. Joseph didn't lift his knees so high or raise his head quite as much.

INFERENCE ABOUT PIERRE AND JOSEPH'S RELATIONSHIP: ______________

____

____

Name ______________________ Date ______________

CHEE'S DAUGHTER

Word List

transfigured	forage	compound	zealously
buttes	alien	gaudy	straggly
queue	surmised	cunning	
jerky	flaunting	acrid	
indolence	rakish	banter	

I. Alphabetize the words in the Word List. The first word is done for you.

1. acrid
2. ______________
3. ______________
4. ______________
5. ______________
6. ______________
7. ______________
8. ______________
9. ______________
10. ______________
11. ______________
12. ______________
13. ______________
14. ______________
15. ______________
16. ______________
17. ______________

II. Write the correct word from the Word List to complete each sentence.

1. During the day, the prisoners exercise in a guarded ______________.
2. If you want to survive in the wilderness and you have no food left, you might ______________ for berries and edible plants to survive.
3. After being on a camping and hiking trip to the desert for four days, Belinda's hair was dirty, stringy, and ______________.
4. She was overdressed, with too much jewelry and too many buttons and bows. Her attire was ______________.
5. He felt like he did not belong. He felt like an ______________ in a strange land.
6. Falling in love ______________ her.
7. Though he ______________ rebuilt the walls of the sandcastle after every wave, the incoming tide finally defeated his efforts.
8. The young girl wore cowboy boots and her hair had been tied in a ______________.

Name ______________________ Date ______________

CHEE'S DAUGHTER

Make Inferences

An author provides the descriptions and events for a story and the reader **makes inferences,** or draws conclusions, by using knowledge about life and the world to make sense of the text. Also, the author often does not tell readers exactly what to think about characters and situations so readers must infer by putting together the pieces of information given. For example, in this excerpt from "Chee's Daughter," the author describes a character.

> There was indolence in his walk even though he seemed to hurry, indolence in his cheeks so plump they made his eyes squint, eyes now smoldering with anger.

The author has described the character's walk, face, and emotions. You might infer that the character is very angry and seems to be ready to take some action.

Read the following excerpts from "Chee's Daughter" and make inferences about each character or setting.

1. There was no bluster in his voice today and his face sagged, looking somewhat saddened; . . .

____

____

2. Unfriendliness began to harden in his father-in-law's face.

____

____

3. Through planting time Chee worked zealously and tirelessly. He spoke little of the large new field he was planting because he felt so strongly that just now this was something between himself and the land.

____

____

Name ______________________________ *Date* ______________

NAVAHO CHANT

Word List

curtain	beautiful	Navaho	goods
power	entrance	pollen	chant

I. Write a synonym from the Word List to match each of the following words.

1. drapery ____________
2. lovely ____________
3. resources ____________
4. door ____________
5. capability ____________

II. Fill in the blanks using words from the Word List.

1. The ____________ in the spring makes my eyes feel itchy and my nose get stuffy.
2. The group sang a ____________ to the sun.
3. Most people have jobs where they make ____________ or perform services.
4. Some of the most exceptional rugs in the world are woven by skilled ____________ weavers.
5. Please open the ____________ so the plants can get more light.
6. The foyer was the most magnificent ____________ into a home that I have ever seen.
7. Truly ____________ people have pure hearts and kind ways.
8. Sometimes it takes additional ____________ from the line to win a football game.

Name ______________________________ Date ______________

NAVAHO CHANT

Identify Fact and Opinion

A **fact** is a statement that can be measured or proven; an **opinion** is a statement that tells what a person believes. Sometimes a statement can contain both a fact and an opinion. For example, read this line from the poem, "Navaho Chant":

I arrive at the beautiful goods curtain which hangs at the doorway.

The underlined word shows an opinion, but the rest of the line is a statement of fact.

Write on the line next to each statement if it is a fact, an opinion, or both. Underline any opinion words.

1. My home is beautiful as well as comfortable. ______________
2. There is an acre of grass surrounding our home. ______________
3. Last night three visitors came to our home and enjoyed themselves immensely. ______________
4. The land upon which a home is built is more important than the house itself. ______________
5. The home we lived in last year was not as expensive as our present dwelling, but it was far more cozy. ______________
6. Our home is on Washington Avenue, and it is the oldest building on the block. ______________
7. A brick home is the safest place to be. ______________
8. My home is made of several different natural materials including brick, wood, and stone. ______________
9. The "Navaho Chant" is an appealing poem which tells about the home of the White Corn Boy. ______________
10. Although my home is attractive, the surrounding area is truly an eyesore. ______________

Name ______________________________ *Date* ______________

THE GOLD MEDAL

Word List

rebelliously	jutting	resignedly	cordial
flurry	indignant	somberly	dismaying
genuine	pert	excavation	flailing
giddy	propel	quavery	tarpaulin
treading	gingerly	Labradors	litter
dappling	pigeonhole	regiment	reluctantly
forlorn	eiderdown quilt	cottonwood	ingloriously
pelt	absorbed	bewildered	

I. Write a word from the Word List to match each definition.

1. deeply interested ____________
2. real ____________
3. hole made by digging ____________
4. push forward ____________
5. group or bunch of spots ____________
6. small compartment in a desk ____________
7. waving wildly ____________
8. animal fur ____________
9. warm; friendly ____________
10. lightheaded ____________

II. Complete these sentences with words from the Word List.

1. He handled the fragile vase ____________ to avoid breaking it.
2. The ____________ of newborn pups was nestled beside its mother.
3. In a ____________ of writing activity, he completed all of his homework, worked on a novel, and began a short story.
4. To protect the playing field from rain, the maintenance workers covered it with a ____________ .
5. The homework ____________ everyone; no one could understand it.

Name ______________________ Date ____________

THE GOLD MEDAL

Use Connotations

The **connotation** of a word suggests feelings associated with the word. Some words have positive connotations and others have negative connotations. By recognizing the connotation of a word you can infer the opinion that it suggests. Here are two examples:

POSITIVE CONNOTATION: Amanda Dawson was *slender*. (Slender suggests a positive opinion about her appearance.)

NEGATIVE CONNOTATION: Amanda Dawson was *skinny*. (Skinny suggests a negative opinion about her appearance.)

Underline the words that have a positive or negative connotation in each excerpt from the story, "The Gold Medal," and answer the questions that follow.

1. Amanda Dawson—tall for her years, a little thin, leggy as a newborn colt.

What kind of opinion does this statement suggest about Amanda's appearance?

____

____

2. Her protest roused the old lady to a flurry of shrill, bird-like cries.

What opinion does this suggest about the old woman?

____

____

3. Mom would split a seam if she even suspected Amanda of speaking up like that, pert and sassy!

What is Mom's opinion of the way Amanda spoke?

____

____

4. When the bell summoned her back to class, Amanda reluctantly joined the hurrying, chattering crowds in the hall.

What is Amanda's opinion of school?

____

____

Name ______________________ Date ______________

FOUR SKINNY TREES

Word List

pointy	**raggedy**	**appreciate**	**ferocious**
concrete	**violent**	**tulips**	**despite**

I. Match each word in the left column with its definition in the right column.

1.	pointy	____	**a.**	lily-like flowers
2.	raggedy	____	**b.**	pavement
3.	appreciate	____	**c.**	with sharp angles
4.	ferocious	____	**d.**	in spite of
5.	violent	____	**e.**	unkept and poor-looking
6.	tulips	____	**f.**	fierce
7.	despite	____	**g.**	be grateful for
8.	concrete	____	**h.**	furious; uncontrolled

II. Write the word from the Word List that best completes each sentence.

1. We surely do ______________ all the flowers you sent to the hospital.

2. The roaring lions with the sharp teeth seemed much too ______________ to be trained to dance on their hind legs.

3. Mr. Vaughn has sharp facial features, and all his children have ______________ noses just like his.

4. The ______________ storm struck without warning and leveled half the town.

5. Luckily, he had his helmet on when his head struck the ______________ sidewalk.

6. She slept until noon ______________ the loud buzzing of her alarm clock.

Name ______________________________ Date ______________

FOUR SKINNY TREES

Identify Main Idea

Every piece of writing has at least one **main idea** that is strengthened by the details in the paragraphs or stanzas of the selection. Each paragraph or stanza also has its own main idea that is supported by details. Being able to identify and understand the main idea of a paragraph or stanza helps you understand the main idea of the whole selection.

I. Read all of the sentences in each group. Then label each as either *MI* (MAIN IDEA) or *SD* (SUPPORTING DETAIL).

1. a. They are the only ones who understand me. ____

b. I am the only one who understands them. ____

c. Four skinny trees with skinny necks and pointy elbows like mine. ____

2. a. They send ferocious roots beneath the ground. ____

b. They grow up and they grow down and grab the earth between their hairy toes and bite the sky with violent teeth and never quit their anger. ____

c. This is how they keep. ____

3. a. When I am too sad and too skinny to keep keeping, when I am a tiny thing against so many bricks, then it is I look at trees. ____

b. Four who grew despite concrete. ____

c. Four who reach and do not forget to reach. ____

d. Four whose only reason is to be and be. ____

II. Based on the excerpts above, what is the main idea of the whole selection?

____

____

____

____

____

____

Name ______________________________ Date ______________

TA-NA-E-KA

Word List

virtue	heritage	nuzzle	stake out
horrendous	shrewdest	endurance	omelet
dialect	skirmish	confide	ritual
marina	ordeal	traditional	

I. Complete the story by writing words from the Word List.

Sgt. Ray Tropeano was a good detective. But then, being a good cop was a part of his (1) ____________ . His father, grandfather, and great grandfather all had been policemen in their day. They each had amazing physical (2) ____________ to withstand the demands of serving on the New York City police force, and each had seen the (3) ____________ results of crime in the big city. Each had survived the (4) ____________ and had, in fact, won many medals for bravery. But Ray was considered the (5) ____________ of them all. In fact, he was so clever that he had never failed to catch the crook.

II. Write the correct word to complete each sentence.

1. All of the dogs I have ever known like to ____________ people with their cold and wet noses.

2. The old gold miners used to ____________ their gold claim, by roping off the area they were mining.

3. My boat, *Easy Ride,* was docked in the ____________ .

4. The eggs can be found in the kichen in the ____________ pan.

5. It was hard to understand him because of his unfamiliar ____________ .

Name ________________________________ Date ________________

TA-NA-E-KA

Recognize Facts that Support Opinions

When you read an opinion, often you will find facts that support the opinion. For example, here is an opinion about Grandfather in the story, "Ta-Na-E-Ka":

Grandfather was a traditional man with old-fashioned ideas.

Which of these facts support this opinion and which do not?

1. He still wore handmade beaded moccasins instead of shoes.
2. He kept his iron-gray hair in tight braids.
3. His name was Amos Deer Leg.

Fact 1 and 2 support the opinion. Fact 3 has nothing to do with it, although it is a fact about Grandfather.

Read the following opinions. Put a check next to the facts that support each opinion.

1. Grandfather was a brave warrior.

____ a. Grandfather was one of the last living Indians who actually fought against the U.S. Cavalry.

____ b. He was wounded in a skirmish at Rose Creek.

____ c. He spoke English only with white men.

2. The Kaw Indian tribe was fair to its women.

____ a. Unlike most other Sioux tribes, the Kaw allowed men and women to eat together.

____ b. Ta-Na-E-Ka means flowering of adulthood.

____ c. Girls as well as boys were required to go through Ta-Na-E-Ka.

3. Ta-Na-E-Ka was a dangerous and exciting time during Grandfather's day.

____ a. We were sent naked into the wilderness without so much as a knife.

____ b. Many didn't return.

____ c. Today we are barefoot and in bathing suits.

Name ______________________ *Date* ______________

DEAD AT SEVENTEEN

Word List

agony	dedicated	wheedled	tradition
successor	saturated	column	statistic
mangled	sympathy	casket	
fatalities	ordeal	overwhelmed	

I. Write the word from the word list that has the same meaning as each word.

1. deaths ____________

2. coffin ____________

3. soaked ____________

4. pain ____________

5. mutilated ____________

6. overcome ____________

II. Write the word from the Word List that best completes each sentence.

1. Matthew ____________ his poem to his father.

2. Being in a car accident is a terrible ____________ .

3. After Paul Bryant's death, Ray Perkins was chosen as his ____________ .

4. She was ____________ by the generosity of her students.

5. I was persistent and I ____________ the use of the car from my mom.

III. Write a brief story using at least five words from the Word List.

____

____

____

____

____

____

Name ______________________ Date ____________

DEAD AT SEVENTEEN

Recognize Valid Opinions

To evaluate whether an opinion is valid, check for supporting facts. For example, read this excerpt from "Dead at Seventeen":

> It doesn't matter how the accident happened. I was goofing off—going too fast, taking crazy chances. But I was enjoying my freedom and having fun.

Which opinion do these facts support?

A. The storyteller was a careful driver.
B. The storyteller was a careless driver.

Facts such as goofing off, going too fast, and taking chances support Opinion B.

Read these excerpts, and answer the questions.

1. After the car crash: "Suddenly I awakened. It was very quiet. A police officer was standing over me. I saw a doctor. My body was mangled. I was saturated with blood. Pieces of jagged glass were sticking out all over. Strange that I couldn't feel anything."

Which is a valid opinion based on the facts in the excerpts? ____
A. Being in a car crash is an unusual way to die.
B. Being in a car crash is a gruesome way to die.

Which facts support the valid opinion?

____

____

2. "The funeral was weird. I saw all my relatives and friends walk toward the casket. They looked at me with the saddest eyes I've ever seen. Some of my buddies were crying. A few of the girls touched my hand and sobbed as they walked by."

Which is a valid opinion based on the facts in the excerpt? ____
A. The funeral of a young boy is a tragic and sorrowful experience.
B. The funeral of a young boy is a common experience.

Which facts support that opinion?

____

____

Name ______________________________ *Date* ______________

THANK YOU, M'AM

Word List

slung	**stoop**	**suede**	**half nelson**
whereupon	**frail**	**plate**	**barren**

I. Write the words in the Word List in alphabetical order. The first one is done for you.

1. barren **4.** ______________ **7.** ______________

2. ______________ **5.** ______________ **8.** ______________

3. ______________ **6.** ______________

II. Write the word from the Word List that best completes each sentence.

1. For her birthday, Tina got a beautiful purse made of black ______________ .

2. The woman had become quite ______________ as a result of her illness.

3. The yard was ______________ ; there were no trees or flowers anywhere.

4. Yoshi dragged his little brother across the lawn by putting a ______________ about his neck.

5. Jenny carried the briefcase strap ______________ across her shoulder.

6. Rupa got a new car, ______________ she stopped taking the bus to work.

7. Paul's apartment had such a small kitchen that he had only one ______________ .

8. After supper, the family liked to sit on the ______________ and tell stories.

Name ______________________ *Date* ______________

THANK YOU, M'AM

Make Predictions

You can begin **making predictions**, or thinking about what might happen next, from the minute you begin a story or book. Ask yourself: What does the title suggest? Are there any illustrations that give clues about what will happen? What might happen to the characters described in the beginning of the story?

Think about the beginning of "Thank You, M'am" when a boy tries to steal a woman's purse. You may have used what you knew about thieves to predict that the boy is headed for trouble.

However, good readers revise their predictions as new information is presented. As you continued to read "Thank You, M'am," your predictions likely changed. When the woman did not turn him in, but rather befriended him, you may have revised your predictions.

Read the title of a short story below. Make a prediction about the story based on the title. Then read each excerpt and revise your prediction based on each new piece of information.

1. "Marathon Woman"

PREDICTION: ______________________

____

2. Juanita wasn't sure if she could outlast the other marathoners; certainly Jolie didn't think so.

REVISED PREDICTION: ______________________

____

3. When the rain began, the mud splattered everywhere. She wondered whether the other racers were feeling as though they too could slip at any moment; they would find themselves in an out-of-breath heap, and the race would be over for them. The elbow she had sprained last year was beginning to ache, but she just kept fighting to finish the race.

REVISED PREDICTION: ______________________

____

4. Finally, the race was over. Juanita finished with mud in her hair and up her arms, sweat dripping from her body, and tears streaming from her eyes. Her wheelchair was filthy but she'd kept spinning the wheels. What would Jolie say now?

FINAL PREDICTION: ______________________

____

Name ______________________ Date ____________

FOUR HAIKU/A BEE THUMPS

Word List

interior	hollow	waterfall
reveals	sill	

I. Write a word from the Word List that could replace the underlined words in each sentence.

1. The girl shows us where her house is hidden. ____________
2. When we saw the inside of the house, our jaws dropped. ____________
3. Plants covered the window ledge. ____________
4. The sound of a river with running water dropping into a pool filled our ears. ____________
5. The tree was rotted and a squirrel lived in the open area in the middle. ____________

II. Write the antonym from the Word List that is the opposite of each word.

1. hides ____________
2. solid ____________
3. exterior ____________

III. Write a paragraph using each of the words in the Word List.

Name ______________________________ Date ______________

FOUR HAIKU/A BEE THUMPS

Identify Fact and Opinion

Poetry, as well as prose and nonfiction writing, may contain lines that are **facts, opinions,** or both. Facts can be proven, opinions cannot; poems may contain both.

Write whether each line of poetry is a fact, opinion, or both. Circle the words that demonstrate your choice for each.

1. Here … there …
the sound of waterfall is heard— ____________

2. … that open mouth
reveals your whole interior … ____________

3. Young leaves make Spring a thing of beauty ____________

4. The bee,
a silly insect,
stings by nature ____________

5. A bee thumps against the dusty window ____________

6. How horrible
this season when
creepy crawly things come out ____________

7. A worm
cut in half
two worms ____________

8. Caterpillar no longer
a butterfly instead
more lovely overhead ____________

9. With the rain
soon comes
happiness and flowers ____________

Name ______________________________ *Date* ______________

STARVATION WILDERNESS

Word List

muskrat	**toboggan**	**stupor**	**foolhardy**
belt	**habitation**	**bannock**	**charred**
bedroll	**thrive**	**confirm**	**snare**
carcass	**hoard**	**scrawny**	**spellbinding**
douse	**grouse**	**presence**	
shoot	**cuddling**	**gag**	
scow	**parka**	**dwindle**	

I. Complete these sentences with words from the Word List.

1. Although Mike was usually a good outdoor cook, this time he ____________ the steaks because the fire was too hot.

2. People who believe a disaster is going to happen often ____________ food and supplies to survive the catastrophe.

3. As the days went by, their supply of food seemed to ____________.

4. She started to choke and ____________ on the meat.

5. A receptionist's job includes calling patients to ____________ their appointments.

II. Circle the letter of the word that best completes each sentence.

1. The ____ of forest land that surrounded the city was full of pines and firs.

a. scow b. belt c. bedroll

2. Campers sometimes sleep in a ____, which may consist of blankets or a sleeping bag.

a. bedroll b. hoard c. snare

3. One way to break up a cat fight is to ____ the cats with water.

a. scow b. douse c. confirm

4. For children to ____ they must have food, shelter, clothing, and, equally important, lots of love.

a. douse b. snare c. thrive

Name ______________________________ *Date* ______________

STARVATION WILDERNESS

Summarize

As you read a story, it is helpful to **summarize**—restate what has happened—to recall the events in the story so far. Often it is necessary to reread, or skim, a passage or story to recall the most important events. A summary does not include every detail, just the basic information about the main characters, the setting, and the problem. For example, a summary of the beginning of "Starvation Wilderness" might read:

> At the beginning of this true adventure, the narrator, her husband, Walter, and their six-month-old daughter, Olive, set out to trap muskrats and other animals in Canada's Far North. The area in which they camp is rich in fur-bearing animals but lacking in game. Their food supply dwindles dangerously low; thus, they call the area Starvation Wilderness.

1. Write a summary for pages 382–385 of "Starvation Wilderness." Include the basic information on what the main characters do or need, where they go (the setting), and how they are trying to solve the problem.

____

____

____

____

2. Write a summary for pages 386–391 of "Starvation Wilderness." Include how the characters solve their problem and what they learn along the way.

____

____

____

____

Name ______________________ Date ______________

DREAMS/UNTITLED/SYMPATHY

Word List

barren	**core**	**carol**	**bruised**
plea	**sore**	**bosom**	**flings**

I. Write a word from the Word List to match each definition.

1. chest ____________

2. center ____________

3. throws wildly ____________

4. song ____________

5. in pain ____________

6. sterile ____________

7. injured ____________

8. appeal ____________

II. Write the letter of the best definition for each underlined word as it is used in the sentence.

____ **1.** The land appears barren in winter without the greenery.

a. ugly b. cold c. bare

____ **2.** We made a plea for the bird's release, but it was to no avail.

a. plan b. threat c. appeal

____ **3.** The strains of carols filled the air as the group continued down the street.

a. songs b. chattering c. violins

____ **4.** His love of freedom came from the core of his heart.

a. top b. depth c. love

____ **5.** She was bruised when she tripped on the rug and fell down the stairs.

a. battered b. burned c. cold

Name ______________________ Date ______________

DREAMS/UNTITLED/SYMPATHY

Analyze Figurative Language

Poets use **figurative language** such as metaphors—comparisons—to bring their writing to life. Sometimes a metaphor can make a concept that is difficult to describe clear and meaningful to readers. Langston Hughes expresses his feelings about the concept of dreams and goals by using metaphors in "Dreams" in the lines:

"Life is a broken-winged bird/That cannot fly."
and
"Life is a barren field/Covered with snow."

Langston Hughes compares life without dreams to a broken-winged bird and to a barren field. To analyze these comparisons, think about what message Langston Hughes is trying to send. For example, your analysis might suggest that Hughes is saying that if you lose your dreams, you will be kept from doing what you are meant to do in life.

Analyze these metaphors by explaining what the author may have been trying to express.

1. Life is a carnival ride. ______________________

____

____

2. Love is a spaceship into the unknown. ______________________

____

____

3. Dreams are shards of a broken vase. ______________________

____

____

4. Dreams are sunshine and fireworks. ______________________

____

____

5. Poetry is music. ______________________

____

____

Name ______________________________ Date ______________

AMIGO BROTHERS

Word List

amigo	tenement	sparring	negative
bout	awesome	pensively	elimination
barrage	psyching	torrent	welterweight
lust	unbridled	demolish	devastating
perpetual	improvised	bilingual	blare
dignitary	bedlam	clarity	coursing
nimble	game	evading	dispelled
mingle	superimposed	restrained	wary

I. Write a word from the Word List to match each definition.

1. causing incredible wonder ______________
2. a fight ______________
3. quick and accurate ______________
4. boxing with another for practice ______________
5. thoughtfully ______________
6. important person ______________
7. weight class in boxing ______________
8. huge number, as in blows ______________
9. make a loud noise ______________
10. crush to pieces ______________

II. Write a word from the Word List to complete each sentence.

1. The boys lived for the day they would move from the ______________.
2. The jazz musicians ______________ notes they felt should be played.
3. Spring seemed ______________; it was rainy for months and months.
4. She spoke two languages so she got the ______________ part in the play.
5. The high winds were able to ______________ the building in minutes.

Name ______________________________ Date ______________

AMIGO BROTHERS

Recognize Changes in Relationships

Often a relationship between characters starts out one way and changes during the course of the story. Such is the case in the story, "Amigo Brothers." Read this excerpt:

> Antonio Cruz and Felix Varga were both seventeen years old. They were so together in friendship that they felt themselves to be brothers.

In this excerpt, the author directly states the relationship of close friendship between the two characters. But this relationship does not remain the same throughout the story.

Answer the questions about these excerpts from "Amigo Brothers."

> Now, after a series of elimination bouts, they had been informed that they were to meet each other in the division finals. ... the winner to represent the Boys Club in the Golden Gloves Championship Tournament.
>
> The two boys continued to run together along the East River Drive. But even when joking with each other, they both sensed a wall rising between them.

1. In the beginning of the story the boys were close friends. How is their relationship the same now? How has it changed?

____

____

2. Why did the boys' relationship change? ______________________________

____

> "You ain't worried, are you?" Tony asked.
>
> "No way, man," Felix laughed out loud. "I got too much smarts for that. I just think it's cooler if we split right here. After the fight, we can get it together again like nothing ever happened."

3. Are Tony and Felix still friends? How can you tell? ______________________________

____

4. How is their relationship different from the close friendship they had in the beginning? ______________________________

____

Name ______________________________ *Date* ______________

ON THE LEDGE

Word List

leaned	**ledge**	**Sergeant**	**inching**
damp	**waver**	**gripped**	**noonday**
dizzy	**faint**	**waver**	
drained	**swung**	**gasped**	

I. Write the word from the Word List that best matches each definition.

1. move in an unsteady way ______________
2. title for a particular rank of police officer ______________
3. moved in a broad arc ______________
4. held firmly ______________
5. bent or inclined ______________
6. fall over ______________
7. twelve o'clock in the daytime ______________
8. faded, tired ______________
9. moving slowly ______________
10. a bit wet ______________

II. Write the word from the Word List that best completes each sentence.

1. The bug began ______________ its way across the picnic table.
2. The crowd ______________ as the man jumped from the burning building.
3. The only way the robber could escape was to crawl along a narrow ______________ running around the apartment building.
4. After spinning on his skates, Dom felt ______________ .
5. The hiker's steps began to ______________ as he walked across a narrow bridge made of just one log.

Name ______________________ Date ____________

On the Ledge

Infer Cause and Effect

In short stories, cause-and-effect relationships are sometimes not stated directly. You must infer why something has happened or what has happened. Read this excerpt from the story, "On the Ledge."

> Eight feet to his left, on a narrow ledge, stood a young man with frightened eyes. …
>
> "Take it easy fella," Gray said. The youth was about the size of his own 17-year-old son.

Why is Gray so concerned about the young man? There are two causes for his concern: He doesn't want the boy to get hurt, and the boy reminds him of his own son.

Read the excerpts and answer the questions.

1. Gray took off his cap and mopped his forehead. His head was wet and sticky. His damp shirt stuck to his back.

   What can you infer is causing Gray to sweat so heavily?

   ____

2. Looking at the youth, Gray was surprised at the sudden change. Walter's face now looked gray. His knees were shaking.

   "Hang in there, Walter," Gray said. He tried to keep his voice calm.

   What can you infer was the reason Gray tried to keep his voice calm?

   ____

   ____

3. Morely reached out the window and grabbed Gray's left leg. Gray knelt on the ledge just six inches wide. He did not look down. He began inching his way toward Walter.

   What can you infer is the reason Gray did not look down?

   ____

   ____

Name ______________________ *Date* ______________

Terror in the North

Word List

Seattle	**bearing**	**catastrophe**	**frail**
jutted	**extreme**	**figurine**	**grimly**
concentrate	**self-conscious**	**pilings**	**rampage**
blurted	**eventually**	**stress**	**tidal wave**

I. Unscramble each word in the left column. Then write the letter of the correct definition next to each unscrambled word.

1. garampe ______________ ____ **a.** very great

2. grabine ______________ ____ **b.** said suddenly

3. meetrex ______________ ____ **c.** a sudden, horrible disaster

4. drubtle ______________ ____ **d.** wild outbreak

5. porthestaca ______________ ____ **e.** advancing rapidly

II. Circle the letter of the word that best completes each sentence.

1. The peninsula ____ from the land into the ocean.

a. jutted b. blurted c. stress

2. The ____ held up the pier and served as its foundation.

a. pilings b. figurine c. stress

3. Mei Ling was very ____ and embarrassed in front of people she did not know.

a. extreme b. self-conscious c. frail

4. The beautiful ____ fell to the floor and broke into a thousand pieces.

a. rampage b. figurine c. pilings

5. Under ____, because they had not slept in days, the team played poorly.

a. stress b. frail c. grimly

Name ______________________________ Date ______________

TERROR IN THE NORTH

Understand the Sequence of Events

Knowing the sequence of events is crucial to understanding the plot of a story. Events are not always written in the same order in which they occur. For example, in this paragraph, which happened first, the party or the hurricane?

> The hurricane was one of the worst storms Heather had ever witnessed. For some reason it reminded her of the night she had been at a party with Josh.

Although the hurricane is mentioned first, the party actually occurred before the hurricane.

Read these excerpts from "Terror in the North," and complete the activities.

1. She was not an Alaskan in any sense of the word. She had, in fact, arrived only a few months before, to live with her aunt and uncle after her mother had died.

Write the numbers from 1–3 in the order in which the events took place.

____ She lived with her aunt and uncle.

____ She arrived in Alaska.

____ Her mother died.

2. Stina's throat was hot and dry. But her legs could still move, and that was what counted. She handed Dan the baby and began to climb up onto the rooftop. She saw the towering wall of water bearing down on them. Two minutes later it struck the Stetsons' house, tearing it to pieces. The garage they had been on top of, only minutes before, went next.

Write the numbers from 1–5 in the order in which the events took place.

____ Stina climbed up onto the rooftop.

____ Dan and Stina were on the garage.

____ The water struck the Stetsons' house.

____ Stina handed the baby to Dan.

____ The water struck the garage.

Name ______________________ *Date* ______________

THE SECRET LIFE OF WALTER MITTY

Word List

referendum	**rakishly**	**corborundum**	**craven**
initiative	**auxiliary**	**distraught**	
derisive	**inscrutable**	**haggard**	

I. Write the word from the Word List that matches each definition.

1. right to vote on laws ______________
2. the right to introduce an idea for a law ______________
3. insulting ______________
4. hard substance ______________
5. additional ______________
6. incomprehensible ______________
7. looking tired ______________
8. worried ______________
9. fashionably ______________
10. fearful ______________

II. Complete each sentence with a word from the Word List.

1. The dog was fierce, and her reaction to it was ______________.
2. Losing the game was a real blow and she was ______________ for days afterward.
3. Alex proposed the ______________ to the town council.
4. Her comments were ______________ and hurtful.
5. The ______________ cable connected the printer to the network.
6. Tina's appearance was ______________ after working on the yard all day.

Name ______________________________ *Date* ______________

THE SECRET LIFE OF WALTER MITTY

Identify Cause and Effect

To identify the **cause** of an event ask yourself *why* the event occurred. To identify the **effect**, ask what *happened*? Read the following excerpt from "The Secret Life of Walter Mitty" and identify the cause and the effect:

> Walter Mitty reached in a pocket and brought out the gloves. He put them on, but after she had turned and gone into the building and he had driven on to a red light, he took them off again.

CAUSE: She had turned and gone and could no longer see him.

EFFECT: He took off his gloves.

Read the excerpts. Identify a CAUSE and EFFECT in each.

1. Once he had tried to take his chains off, outside New Milford, and he had got them wound around the axles. A man had had to come out in a wrecking car and unwind them, a young, grinning garageman.

CAUSE: ______________________________

EFFECT: ______________________________

2. In a way he hated these weekly trips to town—he was always getting something wrong.

CAUSE: ______________________________

EFFECT: ______________________________

3. An excited buzz ran around the courtroom. The Judge rapped for order.

CAUSE: ______________________________

EFFECT: ______________________________

4. We have shown that the defendant could not have fired the shot. We have shown that he wore his right arm in a sling on the night of the fourteenth of July.

CAUSE: ______________________________

EFFECT: ______________________________

Name ______________________ Date ____________

from I HAVE A DREAM

Word List

frustrations	**prodigious**	**creed**
self-evident	**Gentiles**	**hamlet**

I. Write a word from the Word List to match each definition.

1. people who are not Jewish ____________
2. great; huge ____________
3. unhappy feelings that come from not being able to reach one's goals ____________
4. very small village ____________
5. needing no proof; obviously true ____________

II. Complete each sentence with a word from the Word List.

1. A ____________ weight was removed from my shoulders when she offered to help.
2. When we were in Germany, we visited the ____________ where my great-grandfather was born.
3. I am experiencing many ____________ in my effort to learn advanced math.
4. The right of every person to be free is ____________ .
5. Dr. King called on Jews and ____________ to join hands and work together.

III. Write a paragraph that describes a situation that includes one or more of the vocabulary words.

____

____

____

____

____

____

Name ______________________________ Date ______________

from I HAVE A DREAM

Identify Main Idea and Supporting Details

The **main idea** of a passage is the general point the author is communicating. **Supporting details** are those details that are related to the main idea. Sometimes the main idea is stated directly; sometimes you must infer the main idea. In the following excerpt from "Martin Luther King, Jr." the main idea is stated directly:

> As he continued the fight against racial injustice, Dr. King went to jail more than 30 times; his home was bombed and shotgunned; and he himself was slugged, stabbed, and stoned. Although King refused to use or advocate violence, he himself was a continual victim of violence, even to his death.

The last sentence is the main idea. The examples of violence are the supporting details.

Read all of the sentences in each group and determine what topic they address. Then label each as one of the following: (MI) MAIN IDEA; (SD) SUPPORTING DETAIL; (IR) IRRELEVANT DETAIL

1. a. Atlanta, Georgia, is the birthplace of Martin Luther King, Jr. ____

b. Atlanta is the leading industrial center of the southeastern United States. ____

c. There are more than 1,500 manufacturing plants in Atlanta. ____

d. Products manufactured in Atlanta include airplanes, automobiles, chemicals, furniture, and steel. ____

e. Atlanta was originally founded as Terminus in 1837. ____

2. a. Memphis, Tennessee, is the home of several great American memorials. ____

b. Martin Luther King, Jr., was assassinated in Memphis. ____

c. Memphis is the site of Graceland, the mansion and memorial gravesite of Elvis Presley. ____

d. Memphis is the largest city in Tennessee. ____

e. There are two memorials to Dr. Martin Luther King, Jr., in Memphis. ____

Name ________________________________ Date ________________

Warrior Song I/Warrior Song II/ Song of Failure/War Song

Word List

circumvent	**roam**	**warrior**	**vanish**
avoid	**fled**	**failure**	

I. For each word below, write its antonym from the Word List.

1. peacekeeper ____________

2. confront ____________

3. stayed ____________

4. appear ____________

5. success ____________

II. Write the letter of the word that best replaces the underlined words in each sentence.

a. avoid **b.** roam **c.** circumvent **d.** warrior **e.** failure

____ **1.** The only way to get to the sinking ship was to circle around the small island.

____ **2.** The fences allow the horses to move around freely within a certain area.

____ **3.** Some of life's best lessons are learned from being unsuccessful.

____ **4.** As the fighter prepared for battle, his blood started rushing through his veins.

____ **5.** The driver had to slam on the brakes to keep from hitting the girl on the bike.

III. On a the lines below, write five sentences using words from the Word List.

____

____

____

____

____

Name ______________________________ *Date* ______________

WARRIOR SONG I/WARRIOR SONG II/ SONG OF FAILURE/WAR SONG

Recognize Similarities in Poetry

Poems can be similar in a number of ways. Here are some examples of similarities poems might share:

Same style: For example, rhyme and rhythm

Same theme: For example, love or death

Same tone: For example, somber or humorous

Reread these poems from this unit and answer the questions.

Song of Failure

A wolf
I considered myself.
But the owls are hooting
And the night I fear.

War Song

Soldiers,
You fled,
Even the eagle dies.

1. How are the styles, themes and tones of these two poems similar?

STYLES: ______________________________

____

THEMES: ______________________________

____

TONES: ______________________________

____

No one has found a way to avoid death.
To pass around it;

from Warrior Song I

I shall vanish and be no more,
But the land over which I now roam
Shall remain …

from Warrior Song II

2. How are the styles, themes and tones of the two poems similar?

STYLES: ______________________________

____

THEMES: ______________________________

____

TONES: ______________________________

____

Name ______________________________ Date ______________

ULYSSES AND THE TROJAN HORSE/ ULYSSES MEETS THE CYCLOPS

Word List

Trojan	**shrewdest**	**turmoil**	**siege**
persevered	**reeds**	**emerged**	**image**
cunning	**forges**	**idle**	**thong**
jeered	**maimed**	**soothsayer**	**repentance**
prosperity	**breach**	**coves**	**wiles**
oafs	**lair**	**Zeus**	**thrust**

I. Complete each sentence using a word from the Word List.

1. The war left many soldiers injured and ____________.
2. He loved to swim in the many ____________ around Boston.
3. She resented the constant remarks about feminine ____________. Anyone can be deceitful and manipulative.
4. The fans at the soccer game ____________ at the opponents and taunted them with insults.
5. Of all the men, the ____________ was probably the one who remained silent.

II. Circle the letter of the word that best completes each sentence.

1. He was very ____ in a tricky way.

   a. maimed b. cunning c. emerged

2. When he was around Clarice, his worst personality traits ____.

   a. maimed b. jeered c. emerged

3. Julie wanted to know what would happen to her during her lifetime, so she went to a ____ to find out.

   a. soothsayer b. thong c. Trojan

4. The bear was hidden in its ____.

   a. breach b. coves c. lair

5. Always honored by the Greeks, ____ ruled.

   a. Zeus b. Trojan c. oafs

Name ______________________________ Date ______________

ULYSSES AND THE TROJAN HORSE/ ULYSSES MEETS THE CYCLOPS

Understand Character Relationships

Characters' relationships are a major component of a story. In the story, "Ulysses and the Trojan Horse," relationships between groups of characters underlie much of the action within the story. For example:

> The Greeks cried for revenge. Heroes and warriors from every Greek city and town joined hands against Troy.

In this excerpt the relationship between the people of Greece and the people of Troy is the basis for the entire story.

Read each excerpt. Explain the relationship that is being described or inferred between the characters or groups which follow.

1. Of all the Greek heroes, the wisest and shrewdest was Ulysses, the young king of Ithaca. Yet he did not go willingly to war. No, he would rather have remained at home with his good wife, Penelope, and his son, Telemachus.

ULYSSES, PENELOPE, and TELEMACHUS

____

____

____

2. Fierce battles were fought outside the gates. Some were won by the Greeks, some by the Trojans.

GREEKS and TROJANS

____

____

____

3. "Athena protects us," said the hopeful people of Troy. ... The Palladium was a beautiful statue that stood in the temple of Athena. The Trojans believed that it had a strange power to protect its friends.

ATHENA and PEOPLE OF TROY

____

____

____

Name ______________________ *Date* ______________

ANDRE/FAMILY ALBUM

Word List

stout	**range**	**shields**
fragments	**sprang**	**hibiscus**

I. Write a word from the Word List to match each definition.

1. garden plant or shrub bearing large, showy flowers ______________
2. small parts or pieces ______________
3. having a heavy-set body ______________
4. limits in which an object can be seen, found, or heard ______________
5. defends; protects ______________

II. Write the word from the Word List that best completes each sentence.

1. A sunscreen ______________ a person's skin against receiving too many ultra-violet rays.
2. Since the object was not in my ______________ of vision, I could not see it clearly.
3. Mr. Porter is rather ______________, while his wife is rather thin.
4. When the flowers bloom on my mother's ______________ plant, she shows it to all the neighbors.
5. John ______________ into action when he realized that his car was being broken into.

III. On the lines below, write a sentence for each vocabulary word.

____

____

____

____

____

____

Name ______________________ Date ____________

ANDRE/FAMILY ALBUM

Compare and Contrast Poetry Elements

When you read poetry, there are several elements you can **compare or contrast**, including style, point of view, and topic. Compare the poems by stating how they are similar. Contrast them by telling how they are different.

Reread the poems "Andre" by Gwendolyn Brooks and "Family Album" by Diane Stevenson in your book. Then answer the questions to compare and contrast the following elements.

1. How does the style of the two poems compare?

____

____

2. How does the style of the two poems contrast?

____

____

3. How does the point of view of the two poems compare?

____

____

4. How does the point of view of the two poems contrast?

____

____

5. How does the topic of the two poems compare?

____

____

6. How does the topic of the two poems contrast?

____

____

Name ______________________ Date ______________

BREAD

Word List

windings	bruise	wretched	imprisoned
broth	wearily	pursuer	

I. Write a word from the Word List to match each definition.

1. one who chases another ____________
2. clear soup ____________
3. jailed ____________
4. course of events ____________
5. tiredly ____________

II. Complete each sentence using a word from the Word List.

1. It has been cold and miserable all week long. What did we do to deserve such ____________ weather?
2. His story went through so many ____________, it was hard to follow all the twists and turns.
3. After all the water was added to the soup, all that was left was a thin ____________.
4. The thief disappeared into a movie theater in a last attempt to escape his ____________.
5. The accident caused a large ____________ to her leg.

III. Use the words from the Word List to write a brief paragraph describing the man in the poem "Bread."

____

____

____

____

____

____

Name ______________________ Date ______________

Bread

Identify Setting and Mood

The **setting** of a story or poem often creates the **mood** of the selection. In the poem "Bread," the setting is a prison. This is a fitting setting for the somber mood of the poem. However, sometimes the setting is in direct contrast to the mood.

Identify the setting and mood for each of these excerpts. Then explain how the setting fits or does not fit with the mood of the story. Explain your answers.

1. The trumpets blared and the drums beat at a furious pace. The soldiers marched proudly through the small town. Most of the citizens enjoyed the parade, especially the youngest ones. They shouted and cheered happily. But Frances only stared. No parade could begin to make up for the loss of her husband.

SETTING: ______________________

MOOD: ______________________

EXPLANATION: ______________________

____

____

____

2. "I'd never believe it if I didn't witness it for myself," chuckled Uncle Charley.

"I know. I hope they do it again in the next half of the show," said little Sara. "And thanks so much for taking me to this circus. I don't think I've ever seen anything as funny as 22 clowns squeezing out of one tiny car!"

SETTING: ______________________

MOOD: ______________________

EXPLANATION: ______________________

____

____

Name ______________________________ *Date* ______________

SOMEBODY'S SON

Word List

hunched	**prevails**	**denouement**	**trundled**
asphalt	**wryly**	**careened**	**quaver**
crescendo	**stolidly**	**deftly**	

I. Unscramble each word in the left column. Then write the letter of the correct definition next to each unscrambled word.

1. vareuq	______________	____	**a.**	road pavement
2. endarece	______________	____	**b.**	shake, tremble
3. lundtred	______________	____	**c.**	turned on one side
4. yidstoll	______________	____	**d.**	dully; unemotionally
5. shalpat	______________	____	**e.**	rolled along; moved on wheels

II. Circle the letter of the word that best completes each sentence.

1. In most old cowboy films, the good guy usually ____ over the bad guys.

a. quaver b. prevails c. crescendo

2. If you play an instrument or sing with a group, you need to know that ____ means to get louder.

a. asphalt b. denouement c. crescendo

3. Christopher ____ completed his science project by inventing a clever little machine that feeds the fish in his fish tank twice a day.

a. wryly b. deftly c. stolidly

4. The ____ of the murder mystery was that the butler killed Sir Edward because he loved Lady Florence.

a. denouement b. asphalt c. crescendo

5. The mechanic was ____ over the engine.

a. deftly b. trundled c. hunched

Name ______________________________ Date ______________

SOMEBODY'S SON

Understand Character Relationships

To understand similarities and differences among the characters in a story, compare the characters' relationships. By noting similarities and differences in the relationships you will gain a fuller understanding of the characters.

Read these excerpts from "Somebody's Son," and answer the questions.

David's letter to his mom:

Dear Mom,

If Dad will permit it, I would like to come home. I know there's little chance he will. I'm not going to kid myself. I remember he said once, if I ever ran off, I might as well keep on going. …

Please tell Dad—and I guess this'll make him sore all over again—I'm still not certain that college is the answer for me. I think I'd like to work for a time and think it over.

1. What is David's relationship with his father?

____

____

David riding in a car with a man who picked him up:

"Yeah," the driver was saying now, "I know how it is." The corners of his eyes crinkled as if he were going to smile, but he didn't. "I was out on the same old road when I was a kid. Bummin' around. Lettin' no grass grow under me. Sometimes wishin' it would."

"And then, afterward," David asked. "Did you go back home?"

2. What is David's relationship with the driver?

____

____

3. How is David's relationship with his father different from the relationship he has with the driver?

____

____

Name ______________________ Date ______________

THE MEDICINE BAG

Word List

Sioux	**moccasins**	**Wakantanka**	**sage**
vision quest	**Rosebud Reservation**	**thong**	
bolo tie	**butte**	**tepee**	

I. Write a word or phrase from the Word List that best matches each definition.

1. Native American people of the northern plains of the United States

____

2. an herb used for seasoning ______________

3. man's string tie ______________

4. a small reservation in South Dakota ______________

5. narrow strip of leather ______________

6. top of a steep hill ______________

7. slippers made of leather ______________

8. search for a revelation to aid understanding ______________

II. Complete each sentence with a word or phrase from the Word List.

1. A cone-shaped tent of animal skins used as a shelter by the Plains Indians is called a ______________.

2. When my feet are tired, it feels good to slip into a pair of ______________.

3. While driving through the plains, my family saw a lone elk on the flat top of a ______________.

4. Grandpa told us of the ______________ he took in the forest 50 years ago.

5. ______________ is the creator of the world, according to the Sioux Indians.

III. On a separate sheet of paper, write a paragraph using at least 5 words or phrases from the Word List.

Name ______________________________ Date ______________

The Medicine Bag

Compare and Contrast Character Traits

You can **compare and contrast character traits** by noting similarities and differences among characters. Sometimes characters change within a story and it is important to note these changes in order to follow the plot of the story.

Read these excerpts from "The Medicine Bag," and answer the questions.

1. My kid sister Cheryl and I always bragged about our Sioux grandpa, Joe Iron Shell.

a. What is one similarity between Cheryl and her brother?

____

b. What is one difference between Cheryl and her brother?

____

2. As we supported him up the steps, the door banged open and Cheryl came bursting out of the house. She was all smiles and was so obviously glad to see Grandpa that I was ashamed of how I felt.

What differences can you infer between Cheryl and the narrator?

____

3. Grandpa did most of the talking while my friends were there. I was so proud of him and amazed at how respectfully quiet my buddies were. Mom had to chase them home at supper time. As they left they shook Grandpa's hand …

a. What do the narrator and his friends have in common at this point in the story?

____

b. Compare and contrast the narrator's feelings for Grandpa in the three excerpts on this page.

____

____

Name ______________________________ *Date* ______________

MEDICINE/GRANDFATHER

Word List

clumsily	medicine	weep
withered	unbraided	buried

I. Write the word from the Word List that best matches each definition.

1. deteriorated ____________
2. loose ____________
3. ungracefully ____________
4. cry ____________
5. remedy ____________

II. Use words from the Word List to complete these sentence.

1. Oliver is not very graceful, look how ____________ he dances.
2. Some people have feelings that are ____________ and they don't even know that they have them.
3. Sometimes ____________ can make the difference between life or death.
4. She couldn't wear her hair loose at school, but at home she wore it ____________.
5. The stars were so beautiful she began to ____________ with joy.

III. Write a paragraph in which you use at least four of the words from the Word List.

____

____

____

____

____

____

____

Name ______________________________ Date ______________

MEDICINE/GRANDFATHER

Identify Theme

The **theme** of a poem is its main idea, or what it means. The subject is what the poem is about. The theme of a poem may be about love, justice, happiness, or loss—whatever the poet wants to say about the subject. As you read a poem and try to determine the theme, notice the poet's choice of words and images. Read the following lines of poetry and notice the choice of words.

Love laid his sleepless head
On a thorny rosy bed;
And his eyes with tears were red,
And pale his lips as the dead.

The poet used negative words that give the reader a sense of sadness: *sleepless, thorny, pale,* and *dead.*

Read the following lines of poetry and answer the questions that follow.

With wonderful deathless ditties
We build up the world's great cities,
    And out of a fabulous story
    We fashion an empire's glory:
One man with a dream, at pleasure
    Shall go forth and conquer a crown;
And three with a new song's measure
    Can trample an empire down.

from "Ode" *by* Arthur O'Shaughnessy

1. What is the subject of the poem?

____

2. Are the poet's words generally positive or negative? Give some examples to support your answer.

____

____

3. What is the theme of the poem?

____

____

Name ______________________ *Date* ____________

SOME PEOPLE/MY PEOPLE

Word List

shrivel	**rebuild**	**population**	**proud**
stranger	**thoughtful**	**respectful**	
corral	**fireflies**	**hogans**	

I. Write a word from the Word List to match each definition.

1. a fenced in area for keeping livestock ____________
2. build again ____________
3. carefully decided ____________
4. Navajo houses made of branches, clay, and sod ____________
5. people living in a specified area ____________
6. wither ____________

II. Complete each sentence using a word from the Word List.

1. When you walk with your shoulders straight and your head up you show that you are ____________ of who you are.
2. I had never seen the man before, so there was no way that I would go off with a ____________ just because he told me that he knew my uncle.
3. June is the best time to see ____________. They seem to just cover the grassy areas in the backyard.
4. She handles the sacred things in a ____________ way, using care to show proper regard for them.
5. After the tornado, many families had to ____________ their homes.
6. Lyza lives in a small town where the ____________ is only 365.

Name ______________________ Date ______________

Some People/My People

Make Inferences

Poetry often requires the reader to **make inferences** about a poet's meaning. Poetry often expresses feelings and wishes and the poet doesn't always state the meaning of the poem. Make inferences in poetry by reading the entire poem to pick up as much context as you can. Then look at individual words and phrases and think about how they fit into the whole theme of the poem.

Reread the poem "Some People."

Some People
by Rachel Field

Isn't it strange some people make
You feel so tired inside.
Your thoughts begin to shrivel up
Like leaves all brown and dried!

But when you're with some other ones,
It's stranger still to find
Your thoughts as thick as fireflies
All shiny in your mind!

Answer the following questions to make inferences about the poet's meaning.

1. Who might "some people" be? ______________________

2. How can you feel "tired inside"? ______________________

3. What kinds of thoughts would shrivel up because of another person? ______________________

4. How would "other ones" be able to make your thoughts more plentiful? ______________________

5. Which kind of people do you think the narrator prefers, those described in the first stanza or the second? ______________________

Name ______________________________ *Date* ______________

OTTO/CHRISTMAS MORNING I

Word List

fret	fair	naked	frown
bear	plank	care	
presents	ragdoll	button	

I. Write the word from the Word List that matches each definition.

1. to have concern for ______________
2. become worried or upset ______________
3. without clothing ______________
4. gifts ______________
5. even ______________
6. long, thick board ______________
7. endure; put up with ______________
8. child's toy ______________
9. expression of distaste or disapproval ______________
10. a usually round object used to fasten two parts of a garment ______________

II. Write the word from the Word List that best completes each sentence.

1. Mother told me not to ______________ about my low grade in math.
2. I don't ______________ about getting my feet wet—I just want to get home.
3. I could tell by the ______________ on her face that she was angry.
4. Another ______________ has come off my shirt.
5. Somebody had put a ______________ across the ditch so that we could walk to the other side.
6. I could not ______________ to hear his jokes one more time.
7. Allison was excited about her birthday and all the ______________ she would get.

Name ______________________ Date ____________

OTTO/CHRISTMAS MORNING I

Compare and Contrast Poems

Comparing and contrasting poems can often help you understand them. In "Otto" and "Christmas morning i" there are several ideas which can be compared.

In poetry, the theme may express the poet's values or deep feelings. The subject is what the poem is actually about.

1. What is the subject of these two poems? Is it expressed the same in each? ____________

2. Who is doing the telling? ____________

3. In "Otto," the speaker is sensitive to her father's feelings. Which line in the poem expresses this best? ____________

4. What type of person is the speaker in the first poem? ____________

5. In "Christmas morning i," the speaker has mixed feelings. Explain how you think she feels when she sees what her grandmother is doing. ____________

6. Is the narrator in the second poem as sensitive as the child in the first poem? Explain your decision. ____________

7. What would you say is the financial status of each family? Are they similar or very different? ____________

Name ______________________ *Date* ____________

WHALE HUNTING/LUTHER LEAVITT

Word List

Bering Sea	**blanket**	**hunter**
whaling	**group**	**toss**

I. Write a word from the Word List to match each definition.

1. throw __________
2. going to sea to catch a whale __________
3. person who pursues game for food or sport __________
4. sea near Alaska __________
5. bed covering __________

II. Complete each sentence using a word from the Word List.

1. The __________ is part of the North Pacific Ocean between northeast Siberia and Alaska.
2. We often dine sitting on a __________ on the lawn in the summer.
3. The Inuit are a proud __________ of people.
4. The children enjoyed the blanket __________ .
5. Luther was a __________ of whales.

III. On the lines below, write a description of a whale hunting celebration using words from the Word List.

____

____

____

____

____

____

____

____

Name ______________________ *Date* ______________

Whale Hunting/Luther Leavitt

Identify Cause and Effect

In real life, many things happen for a logical reason. In order to make readers see events as plausible, logical happenings, authors often explain why things happen as they do. **Cause and Effect** is the explanation of what happens and why it happens in a piece of writing.

Read "Whale Hunting" by Sally Nashook Puk and think about what happens (effect) and why (cause).

Whale Hunting

My daddy goes whaling in the Bering Sea
I'm just a girl, he can't take me
My brother joins the whaling group
They caught four this year
for muk-tuk soup.

If you ask yourself, "What happened?" to find the effect, you would probably answer that the narrator's brother got to go whaling instead of her. If you ask yourself, "Why did this happen?" you'd answer that it was because she is a girl.

Reread "Luther Leavitt" and determine the cause and effect of what happens in the poem.

Luther Leavitt

Luther Leavitt is a whale hunter.
last year
they got a whale
we went
to the blanket toss
I never
got a chance to go
on the blanket
cause there were too many kids.

1. What happened? (effect): ______________________

____

2. Why did it happen? (cause): ______________________

____

3. Did the effect seem plausible, given the cause? ______________________

____